# GIRL, GET YOUR $HIT TOGETHER!

#ADULTING **YOUR** WAY

*lisa* CHASTAIN

GIRL, GET YOUR $HIT TOGETHER!

©2017 Lisa Chastain

All Rights Reserved. Printed in the U.S.A.

ISBN-13: 978-1981290130
ISBN-10: 1981290133

All rights reserved. This book or any portion thereof may not be reproduced or used in any manner whatsoever without the express written permission of the publisher except by a reviewer, who may quote brief passages and/or show brief video clips in a review.

Disclaimer: The Publisher and the Author make no representation or warranties with respect to the accuracy or completeness of the contents of this work and specifically disclaim all warranties of fitness for a particular purpose. No warranty may be created or extended by sales or promotional materials. The advice and strategies contained herein may not be suitable for every situation. This work is sold with the understanding that the Publisher is not engaged in rendering legal, accounting or other professional services. If professional assistance is required, the services of a competent professional person should be sought. Neither the Publisher nor the Author shall be liable for damages arising therefrom. The fact that an organization or website is referred to in this work as citation and/or potential source of further information does not mean that the Author or the Publisher endorses the information, the organization or website may provide or recommendations it may make. Further, readers should be aware that internet websites listed in this work may have changed or disappeared between when this work was written and when it is read.

Publishing and Design:

**EPIC AUTHOR PUBLISHING**

Ordering Information: Quantity sales. Special discounts are available on quantity purchases by corporations, associations, and others. For details, contact the publisher at the address above. Orders by U.S. trade bookstores and wholesalers.

Please contact: 800-273-1625 | support@trevorcrane.com | EpicAuthor.com

First Edition

To my SISTERs:

You are more powerful than you can ever imagine.
You make a difference.
You are changing the world.
I believe in you.

# GET THE FREE BOOK BONUSES

WWW.ADULTINGYOURWAY.COM

## lisa CHASTAIN

# DON'T WANT TO WAIT?

MAYBE YOU'RE HERE BECAUSE YOU'RE CURIOUS. Maybe you're here because you've been telling yourself for years that you need to get your $hit together and today is the day that you're ready to do this.

Maybe you're here because things in life are going okay but you know that there are some things you can do better.

Whatever the case, I'm glad you're here.

If you're here because you know that you're ready to make new choices with your money, you're finally ready to live with purpose, and LOVE your life, I invite you to schedule a call with me.

I could have waited until you'd reached the end of the book to make this offer, but here's what I know.

When you're ready, you're ready. This book is a guide, a wealth of information, and I know after reading it you will be making worthwhile and meaningful changes in the direction of your life.

But I don't want you to wait any longer. Today IS the day and if you're ready to take action, and want and need help getting there, let's schedule a call.

Echoing my favorite author Danielle LaPorte, "You're here for a reason."

Don't wait—let's chat for 15 minutes today.

Schedule here: lisachastain.setmore.com

# SISTERS, THIS BOOK IS FOR YOU

I'M SO HONORED YOU'RE HOLDING THIS BOOK in your hands right now.

(Or reading it on your favorite electronic device.)

First, I want you to know you're not alone.

You weren't born knowing anything about money.

And it's not intuitive to know how to change your life either. Everyone can benefit from a little help. (Personally, I like a lot of help.)

I know you want more. I know you have brilliant dreams that are just waiting to be unleashed.

But here's the thing, girl. The first thing you must do is get control of your money.

That may sound weird, but it's the plain truth. It may sound hard to believe, but once you get in control of your money, everything else falls into place. It sifts your mindset, and your confidence, and it's (for lack of a better term) an adult-report card that PROVES to yourself you can do anything.

I know this, because I had to go through a similar journey. And it changed EVERYTHING for me.

Here's what I learned: **Getting in control of your money is the single most important thing you can do.** (Aside from taking control of your health. You better keep yourself healthy and avoid the stuff that you know will hurt you. But that's another subject…)

Look, your "future self" wants and needs you to understand that the decisions you make today WILL impact your future.

We all have a story.

We all have a moment in time or a lesson we refer to when we think about money.

Our beliefs and behaviors came from somewhere. They are not part of WHO YOU ARE… They are just part of your past. They helped you get to "here" and they have served you well. But, what you learned about money when you were a child (right or wrong) affects the decisions you make today. These decisions affect EVERYTHING in your life. Where you go. Who you hang out with. What you buy. What you don't buy. The relationships you have. How you feel about yourself. Your relationship with money affects the inner-self-talk that serves us… or holds us back.

I'm here to help you discover that bringing light to the conscious, and subconscious decisions you used-to-make about money, is key to your transformation. It's the first step in understanding your relationship with money. And I mean that when I say it; you do have a "relationship" with money. Until you get in control of it, it's often a relationship that brings heartache, struggle, and pain. (Maybe you've had a relationship like that with someone in your past? I know I have.)

But once you shine a light on where you've been, you can look forward to your future and understand WHY and HOW you can make decisions to ensure your future is better and brighter.

I often tell my clients, *"The decisions you make today are the ones either your future self will love or hate you for."*

Taking control of your money will stabilize your life. You will feel better as a result, and I promise, your life will get better, day by day. I have clients whose lives drastically improved once they'd taken control of their money. You're going to hear their stories throughout this book. I'll also share with you how controlling my money dramatically impacted my life.

I want you to have everything you want in life. You deserve to have wealth, health, memories, experiences, amazing relationships, and a career you love. You can, and should, have it all.

The best way to build a life you love is to understand the intimate connection between "all" of what you want and your relationship with money.

Again, I'm so honored you chose to join me on this journey and say, "YES" to your future.

I hope with all my heart that you'll find what you need inside this book.

And that you'll take the necessary steps to make your life even more amazing than it already is.

I believe in you, sister.

—Lisa

*I also hope that I'll get the chance to meet you personally very soon.

Always remember that you are incredible, and that you can do ANYTHING!

# TABLE OF CONTENTS

| | |
|---|---|
| Foreword | xv |
| Introduction | 1 |
| **PART I. AWARENESS** | 7 |
|     **Chapter 1:** Who You've Been and How You Got There | 9 |
|     **Chapter 2:** Your Driving Force | 31 |
|     **Chapter 3:** Standing in the Gap | 43 |
| **PART II. ACCEPTANCE** | 57 |
|     **Chapter 4:** Your Hidden Superpowers | 59 |
|     **Chapter 5:** #Visioneering | 67 |
|     **Chapter 6:** Dealing with Haters | 75 |
| **PART III. ALIGNMENT** | 87 |
|     **Chapter 7:** #YouDoYou | 89 |
|     **Chapter 8:** Reckless Vs. Responsible | 99 |
|     **Chapter 9:** The Easy Way | 105 |
| **PART IV. ACTION & ACCOUNTABILITY** | 113 |
|     **Chapter 10:** Be Savage | 115 |
|     **Chapter 11:** Playbook | 125 |
|     **Chapter 12:** Find Your #Tribe | 137 |
| Acknowledgments | 151 |
| Products & Services | 157 |
| About The Author | 159 |

# FOREWORD

YOU'VE JUST MADE A VERY SMART CHOICE to pick up this book. Now, you have to do what most people won't… actually read it.

As a millennial woman, you have the potential (and luckily time on your side) to design the life you want. And with this book, you now have the <u>ability</u> to create financial freedom and as Lisa says, "a life on purpose."

Your job is simply to read this book and put what you learn into action, which is exactly what Lisa has demonstrated for you in her own life and business.

When I first met Lisa, I immediately recognized in her an unbelievable <u>drive</u> and <u>passion</u> to help people and make a huge difference.

At the time, she was struggling with building a successful financial planning business, and my first thought was that the numbers just didn't add up.

Here was a woman who was motivated, committed and willing to do anything to help people… but she wasn't having the success she *should* have been having.

For example, she was recently chosen as team captain to raise money for a local at-risk elementary school and they successfully raised $67,000 in seven days. It didn't make sense that she wasn't able to create the same type of success for herself.

I thought…

This woman is a leader.

*This woman is going to make a GREAT impact.*

*This woman <u>should</u> be successful and <u>MUST</u> be successful… because the world is waiting for her.*

And I was right.

Lisa took a leap of faith (and a big financial risk) to hire me and I have had the honor and privilege to be her business coach over the last year. To put it lightly, she has been a poster child of creating **extraordinary success** and **impact** in an incredibly *short* amount of time.

It wasn't a lack of motivation or willingness to take action that had prevented Lisa from being successful before. What Lisa needed was what every woman needs. She needed the right <u>mentor</u>, a winning <u>mindset</u> and specific <u>strategies</u> to know exactly what to do and how to do it. Then it was game over. She just won.

Through this **amazing** book packed with compelling stories, proven techniques and real-life advice, Lisa is paying it forward. With Lisa as your mentor and guide, you will have everything you need to be financially successful, even if you don't always feel motivated or confident.

**Yes, get ready to win in the game of money and in the game of life.**

Before I became a Business Growth Expert for women, I was a Money Coach and before that, a Certified Financial Planner™ practitioner, so I understand the challenges women face and I also know how necessary it is for you to get the <u>right</u> information and advice, so you can get in control of your money and change your life.

None of the real skills needed to build wealth, make intelligent financial decisions or even manage money on a day-to-day basis are taught in school.

In essence, you were taught to get <u>good</u> grades, get a degree from a <u>good</u> school (which costs an arm and a leg, by the way), get a <u>good</u> job and then somehow **have** enough money to live a <u>good</u> quality of life *now* and **save** enough money to have a <u>good</u> lifestyle in retirement *later*.

However, you may not have been taught (until now that is) to create the life you want. To make conscious and intentional financial decisions… so that you can **do exactly what you want to do** and be **fulfilled** doing it.

*Girl, Get Your $hit Together* gives you the right steps and tools you need to do just that.

Lisa is real with you, talks to you like a true friend and gives you the keys to the kingdom.

What Lisa teaches in this book is that no matter who you are, or where you come from, you can **ALWAYS** turn your reality around, live a life on **purpose** and be **great with your money.**

Lisa shares <u>easy</u> and <u>nontraditional</u> tips and secrets about how to shift from the fear of not having enough money to feeling **confident** and **capable** about making important decisions about money and life.

Her message is perfectly designed to help young Millennial women who are ready to take **action** but who may be unclear of what action to take to <u>transform</u> their own lives.

In this book, Lisa shares detailed examples of the transformation of her clients who have become more demanding of themselves and others, who are paying off debt faster than they could have ever imagined and are working together with other women to create financial success in their lives.

Reading these stories will inspire you to believe that financial freedom IS possible for you, and Lisa walks you through how to do that, every step of the way.

*Girl, Get Your $hit Together* is extremely unique.

It's very different than anything that's out there because Lisa is <u>not just talking about money</u> throughout this book, she talks directly to **you**. This is not your "typical" money management book. Instead, it digs deep into the psyche of **why** you make decisions with your money and **how to** align your purpose with your present-day choices.

It is filled with **honest** and **practical** advice that has been tested in the trenches. It is not theoretical, nor is it filled with advice that is outdated or archaic.

No matter your background or knowledge about money, you can read this book and understand its common sense practical tips, <u>so you can start #adulting and loving your life.</u>

Lisa is a voice of hope for young Millennial women who may feel like they have more choices than they know what to do with and become paralyzed by them.

By reading this book, in lieu of getting the much-too-familiar condition of "analysis paralysis," you will get clear about what matters to you, <u>**uniquely**</u>—and you'll have the **inspiration** and **wisdom** to live your life with <u>purpose</u> and make <u>choices</u> with your money that aligns with you… and you alone.

Remember… money does not have to be complicated!

GIRL, GET YOUR $HIT TOGETHER!

Get ready to start making simple and easy choices <u>without the stress</u>.

***Dive into this book, and treat it like the life-changing resource it truly is.***

—**Robyn Crane**
Speaker, Trainer & Business Growth Expert for Women
#1 International Best-Selling Author of
*Make More Money, Help More People*

INTRODUCTION

# You Don't Know What You Don't Know

*"When You Know Better, You Do Better."*
—Maya Angelou

WHEN YOU DON'T KNOW WHAT YOU'RE DOING, it's easy to let yourself off the hook. How many times have you said, "I don't know how to do this, so I am not going to try it"?

You weren't born knowing anything about money, yet somehow, you're expected to know it all. BUT YOU DON'T. And it's scary, confusing, overwhelming, and rather than DEALING with it, you ignore your money problems. Then things don't get any better. I know you. I get you, because I was you. I was the woman who wanted desperately to get her life together, and I needed major help with my money but I also needed real, honest and practical advice that was RELEVANT to get on the right track.

I needed this book when I was trying to get my sh*t together, so I'm writing this book for you because I spent 20 years searching for answers on how to make money, love money, and LOVE MY LIFE.

This book is for you because I want you to know how to do the same without spending 20 years of your life figuring it out.

When it comes to money, ignorance is not bliss. It's scary.

I feared my fight to be successful was going to be met by a resounding "NO" from everyone, that I truly was destined to be a stay-at-home housewife. I was terrified I was not going to make a difference in this world. It was deep and killing me inside.

## I felt afraid, lost and ashamed.

So, This Book Is Perfect For You If You:

- Get confused and overwhelmed by the thought of money.
- Struggle to get ahead with your money no matter how much you earn.
- Are not making as much money as you would like.
- Hate your job but stay because the money is good.
- Are dissatisfied because you want more and you know you deserve better.
- Are afraid or ashamed to reach for help or tell somebody you need help.

*Know you are not alone. You're in the right place.* And, this book is perfect for you if you're tired of going nowhere month-to-month, and you're ready to get on track with your finances, and with your life! What I share with you is the result of having invested over $100,000 in 20 years and over 1,000 hours of emotional intelligence training. Many things worked. Many things didn't. I learned the hard way. You don't have to. This book can help save you *years* of time and effort.

When I was down to the last of my savings, I was exhausted and I didn't know how to fix what was broken, I knew I needed to reach for help. Reaching out for help was the scariest thing for me to do. That's when I found my coach Robyn. She helped me turn my life around.

I'm glad I invested in the right coaches and mentors to help me transform my life. Not just my money life, but my entire life! Today, I can enjoy the following results in my life: I wake up doing what I love every single day and earn great money doing it. I can provide for my son and take him on vacations. I'm healthier than I have been in 10 years. More importantly, I get to make a difference for people every single day. *This is true for many of my clients, too.*

## WHAT YOU WILL LEARN

In this book, I'm going to share with you my proven 5A Coaching System™ to help you:

- Make more money doing what you love and believe in.
- Find a fulfilling career that pays you what you are worth.
- Contribute to causes you believe in.
- Spend more time with your loved ones; friends and family.
- Enjoy leisurely activities such as travel, relaxation, and the great outdoors.
- Enjoy material pleasures such as having your dream car and home.

You can finally stress less, and live more.

> "Before I met Lisa Chastain, money was a "come in Wednesday night and gone by Thursday" kind of thing. Bills would get paid most of the time but there was never a concept of saving for the future for me and my family. Lisa gave me the tools to not only feel confident with my money, but she also gave me the confidence to talk about money with my husband. We are now on the same page and want the same financial future—I didn't think that would ever be possible! With Lisa's training, we have paid off over $9,000 in debt with a plan to pay off the rest in the near future. Not only are we on our way to financial freedom, I am now in the right frame of mind to start my own business and pursue a career I am truly passionate about!"
> —Sarah, Beauty Consultant, 29

## THE DIFFERENCE

This book isn't just about money. It's about life. You will come to realize money can be a tool to assist you in making your dreams and wishes come true. Money can help you leave a legacy and make a difference on the planet.

> "Lisa Chastain has truly been a lifesaver for me and my business. I left my job prior to meeting her and was struggling to figure out how I was going to make money in my new business. After hiring her, my business launched at a faster pace than I could have imagined bringing in close to $10,000 in just four months! I am learning how to be self-sufficient financially and avoiding making poor financial decisions. Learning about money beliefs, my worth, and redefining my values has elevated my life. Lisa knows her stuff and in months, I have transitioned from a place of scarcity to abundance! I wish I would have met and hired her sooner!"
> —Emily, Owner of Empowered Wellness, 29

# HOW TO USE THIS BOOK

This is the kind of book you can read once, and come back to when you need it. Read chapter by chapter—take action on the exercises and return when you're ready for the next step. If you want to accelerate the results—reach out for help—book your FREE strategy session with me.

Let's get your $hit together!

Lisa Chastain

> *"Lisa Chastain has changed my life. When I met her, I had come to a point where I couldn't focus on anything because twice a month I was dreading getting paid... not because I wasn't making any money but because I didn't have any money. I was drowning in debt. She embraced me and taught me how to let go of my old, depressed world. She helped me rebuild. Lisa taught me how to focus on what my income is, and how can I expand on my talents to make more. I got clear on what I want for my family's future, how to stop spending on stupid $hit (even if it's credit card fees). In just 6-7 months I've paid off $5,000 in credit card debt! Now I'm working toward buying my first home! I am relieved, happy, and grateful and I know that I am enough! I would not be where I am now without her."*
> —Danielle, Business Manager, 33

# PART I.
# AWARENESS

CHAPTER 1

# Who You've Been And How You Got There

---

*"The past teaches us a lesson. The present helps us in our decisions, and the future helps us dream."*
—Unknown

## WHEN I WAS GROWING UP.

BEFORE WE TALK ABOUT YOU, I want you to get to know me, so you understand where I am coming from. But, also how I got here, writing a book to YOU. I want you to know my pain and my struggle because you need to know you're not alone. Money problems suck. I've had plenty of them in my life. I have had great days, and horribly stressful days. I used to beat myself up and not feel worthy of having what I want in life. I have spent my life fighting uphill to get where I am now. When it comes to money, I have messed up royally, time and time again. This is my story I'm grateful to share with you, and I know you have yours.

Once I'm done, we'll be *focusing on you for the rest of the book*.

We will center on what *you* need to know and understand, so you can control your money and live purposefully in a life you love.

# WHAT ABOUT ME

I grew up in small-town Las Vegas. I'm talking when Vegas was an infant, just learning how to walk in the world. I was born in a city I don't recognize today. Dirt roads, horses, fewer than 500,000 people. We lived in the same house for 17 years. My mom stayed home, and my dad worked hard for his money.

My dad was dirt poor as a kid growing up in the back woods of Atlanta, Georgia. His dad was a carpenter and they moved around a lot when my dad was a kid. He has memories of coming home from school and his entire house would be packed into the back of their truck and they would move, constantly. By the time he was a teenager, my great uncle was making a decent living as a stagehand on the Las Vegas strip circa 1950s. My father moved out west to make a better life for himself. I learned from watching him that you have to work hard to have anything worth having. He would work 2-3 days at a time non-stop and then come home and crash. I remember having to be very quiet as a child so we wouldn't wake him up. We were a blue-collar family making ends meet most of our lives. Until retirement, he never made more than $60,000 a year. He and my mom were very smart with their money, pinching pennies and thrift shopping it up when we were kids. As much as I never went without, I learned a lot about money from my parents despite the fact that *they never really talked about money to us.*

I had such respect for my parents that us kids, just did what they said and didn't question how money was handled in the house. I accepted the fact we were on a fixed income, my dad worked hard and we were doing the best we could with money. It wasn't until I went to college that I realized some people had a lot more money than we did. I saw the difference. Girls walking around campus with name brand clothes, driving BMWs. When I saw that, it occurred to me that not everyone had grown up the way we had. When I was in high school, one of the kids in my class had money. I could tell by her clothes and other possessions. But she wasn't the norm. She was the exception. Everyone in our midst budgeted and lived within their means. I never felt like we were poor and we weren't, but money was always tight. Now, you know some of my story. What about yours?

When did you realize what your money beliefs were?

Can you identify a time in your life when you realized your financial situation was different than others?

Growing up, my mom's and dad's attitudes toward money ultimately became the attitude I developed toward money. This is the case for most, if not *all* of us, so it's important to understand what those influential attitudes are. My mom ran our household budget and what I remember most is *there was never enough money*.

We were ALWAYS on a budget, always saving money, and we never spent money on things we didn't need. If it wasn't on sale or at a yard sale mom didn't and won't buy it. She had an accounting background and budgeted the family money down to the very last dime. My mom was always shopping for a deal. After going through similar exercises you'll find in this book, I realized the reason I could or couldn't do things as a child was because of money. I couldn't take school trips, go out to eat, travel anywhere on a plane, buy the electronics we wanted, try a new sport or stay in the sport I loved. Money was the reason given for a "yes" or a "no." It was always about money. Either we could afford to do it, or we couldn't. As you think about how you were raised with money, I invite you to think about what the people around you taught you about money. Were they cheap? Did they spend money like water? I can only imagine what it was like for my father to grow up poor. I know he worked his entire life to provide for his family and to be financially stable. I know my mother made the best and most out of what we had. I also know that I developed my own beliefs and behaviors with money by watching my parents and family with money. You did, too. And it's not until you take a long hard look at how those experiences shaped your relationship with money that you can begin to change what doesn't work for you. Stick with me. I'm going to take you through a series of exercises in this book that will help you distinguish between your money beliefs and those you adopted from other people.

To control your money, it is imperative for you to separate your beliefs from others. That's where the real power comes from.

# I learned that if I wanted anything in life I was going to have to earn it myself.

The urge to earn my own money started young. I remember the first time I was told by my parents I couldn't do something because of money. As a competitive inline roller speed skater, the cost to keep up with my sport was starting to add up with practice, meets, and travel costs. I believe my parents wanted to support me, but because of my dad's limited salary with three kids at home, it just wasn't possible to keep up with the money needed. This is when my hustle began. I babysat, house sat and did anything I could for money starting as young as 10 years old. I was determined even then to get what I wanted. I just knew that I was destined to be the only one in my life to foot the bill for the things I wanted. My dad really tried to support me; he paid for tennis, clarinet and gymnastic lessons but I never heard the end of how much it was putting us out as a family. So, I decided very early on in my life that I was going to handle my finances myself. It wasn't easy, but as I stared my 38th birthday in the face, I was proud of who I'd become.

I want the same for you. I want you to understand where you developed your money beliefs. After figuring that out for myself, I learned to appreciate, and accept the beliefs and behaviors I'm congruent with and leave behind any beliefs and behaviors where I'm not congruent. I know you're going through your own battle of financial independence, and I'm here to tell you that you can have it. It is possible! My book is going to teach you what you need to know. Follow the exercises and most importantly, make an investment of time in yourself, girlfriend. You are worth it one million percent!

The first goal I focus on when I work with new clients is gaining an understanding of my client's behaviors and beliefs about money. After taking the time myself to listen to that internal chatter that exists in my brain, I know there are definite thoughts about money that I inherited from my parents and my past, and I know my clients have developed their own money values, too.

For example, I'll catch myself telling my son, "No, we can't go because we don't have the money." Then I have to stop and think, *the real reason we can't go is because I'm feeling lazy and just don't want to.* My response doesn't always involve money considerations.

We all have inner voices that influence the way we make decisions. Before every major purchase, every time you get stressed out, you will tell yourself internally how you feel about it. As a woman, you've probably gotten good at beating yourself up, too. I audited my own beliefs about money and here are the inner conversations I have (most regularly):

- "Don't ask money for anything and NEVER ask anyone for help."
- "Hard work will pay off."
- "Money doesn't come easily."

- "You must work for money's affection." In other words, "For money to have value you have to work hard for it."
- "You don't need money to be happy."
- "People are the most important parts of our lives."
- "A good, stable job will give you the money you need."
- "There's never enough money (and there never will be enough)."
- "Money isn't worth the trouble and effort."–

Maybe you can relate to some of the above attitudes. Maybe not. The ladies I've met and worked with, will tell me their beliefs and the sayings their parents instilled in them surrounding money. When they think about how they have lived their "money life," their decisions match those sayings.

It's illuminating.

Suffice it to say, we could probably add a few (hundred or so) more sayings to that list.

Here's the way I like to look at it.

I have always been driven in life. Because of how I grew up, I knew if I wanted to do anything, I was going to have to figure out how to pay for it. I was also very resentful toward my parents about our money conversations. I equated their inability to support me financially to their lack of support for me in general. *Money became motivation for me.* My belief about money was that it was the access point for experiences and things in life.

## Money was a gateway for me.

I knew EARLY in my life that if I wanted something I was the one who was going to have to make it happen. I got my first job at 12 as a babysitter. My belief was that I was going to work hard for things, and I proceeded to do that through my 20s. It didn't matter what I did—I was always a "good" girl and an overachiever by many measures.

On one hand, it was useful to have this drive. My work ethic is what it is today because of it. I'm proud of my dedication to work. However, because making money *had* to be hard work, it was exhausting and limited the possibility that money could work for me rather than *me for it*!

I correlated the amount of time and effort I put into my job into how much money I would make. I believed that if I worked hard, I would see the benefit financially. So, I became a slave to my work. I lacked creativity and didn't know there were any other possibilities.

My first job was as a party hostess at the local roller skating rink. I worked long hours and would hustle to make sure my parents were always happy. My work ethic paid off because I made great tips! I worked three jobs in college: as a peer advisor (on campus), in a restaurant as a hostess, and I house sat as much as possible. Yes, I was productive and made decent money, but I felt like I worked all the time. If I took the time to think about how hard I worked, and if I wanted to make better use of my hours, I could probably have found a better paying job where I could have worked less and made MORE money. My self-limiting belief was that I *thought* I had to work 60 hours a week to believe that money was worth anything of value. If I didn't work hard for it, it didn't matter.

*Money and I had a love hate relationship.*

When I have money, I feel like life is good; everything is going to be okay.

When I didn't have money (there were times where I was substantially overdrawn in my checking account), I felt stressed and worried. I lost sleep at night. It didn't feel good to be in that reality. Ever.

If I had money, I didn't worry. I bought things I liked.

If I didn't have money, I was depressed, stressed and always in a hustle to find more money.

Even though I gravitated toward people who had money, at the same time I'd be embarrassed by my clothes, shoes, car, and my unworthiness.

I still battle this internal self-limiting conversation because I have a limiting belief that *I'm not what success looks like*, and that I'm not worthy of financial success.

I had subscribed to the "work hard/play hard" philosophy. If I wasn't in class, I was working and if I wasn't working I was out partying with friends. I would sleep, and repeat 6-7 days a week. It was exhausting. I was out of breath. I have repeated this cycle over and over again in my life. Everyone runs patterns. As you read this part of my story, ask yourself: "Do I know my work and money patterns?"

I would spend my money on other people to compensate for my feelings of being unworthy. When I felt sad or as if there was a void in my life, I would buy gifts and cards for my family. I might go to Hallmark and buy a gift for my mom (a trinket or present she really didn't need) that I thought would make her feel good. And I did the same for my friends, as well as I would overspend on treating for lunches and dinners. Doing that made me feel like I was getting the praise or acknowledgment I so desperately needed.

*No surprise, that in my eyes, I was always broke.*

I didn't have the clothes, the hair and the other things my wealthier friends had, and I felt lesser than in their presence. Complaining wasn't allowed in our household. My mother would tell me to be grateful for what I had and she would shut down any conversations that were difficult. She would tell me that I didn't need money to be happy, which is true, but having money really does help!

When I'd complain about not having enough money, my mom would regularly answer (still does), "You don't need things to make you happy. Your family is what matters most." If I was ever feeling down, she would tell me that I could be "butt ugly," lol. Meaning I should be grateful for the fact I have a pretty face and am attractive. This is how it went; there wasn't room for anything other than gratitude, which kept many feelings pent-up and I would feel unheard.

No matter what I did, I never felt like it was going to be enough because I didn't have enough money—I was constantly comparing myself to other friends who "had money." It was a losing game that damaged my self-esteem.

This became a trend throughout my 20s and 30s before I turned it all around. I would spend mostly on credit cards, and I made those decisions out of emotion. I knew very little about how to use debt responsibly, and had no idea how hard it would actually be to get out of debt, without a strategy in place.

I was never taught how to balance saving with spending. Nor was I taught how to invest and grow my money. I signed up for credit cards as soon as I could and I charged them up fast. In fact, I'm still paying off over $20K in credit card debt that I accumulated in my 20s... mostly on stupid shit (aka – things I don't even want or need today—other than my couch. I really needed my couch).

No one tells you how expensive kids are either. If you're a mom and you're reading this, I feel your pain, sister. Kids are expensive! I had my son at 28 years old. My husband and I were building our careers and lives and thought we were ready to be parents. Wooooo boy, was I wrong! Here's the truth; I was working 60-hour weeks, and my husband, over 80 hours. We were literally burning the candle at both ends, chasing the Joneses, and working so hard, all while trying to raise a very vibrant healthy child. We thought we were invincible. That belief extended to believing we were invincible financially. Money was always coming in, and we were arrogant and believed it always would. I got promotion after promotion and so did my husband.

I spent money on stupid shit like clothes I barely wore... all to impress other people. We were miserable.

To make matters worse, I was chasing an ideal image in my head, chasing the idea of what success looked like rather than defining success for myself. In my early 20s, success looked like a white picket fence, being married with 2.5 children, and owning a perfectly clean home with a closet filled with name brand clothing. My reality of what I had envisioned turned out differently. My husband and I racked up thousands of dollars of credit card debt on clothes, shoes, jewelry, and expensive haircuts. What I didn't know was that pursuing the ideal image I'd conjured in my head and comparing my life against it was a losing game.

Then, during a time where my husband and I should not have been homeowners, we stretched ourselves and bought a house. That house ended up costing us thousands of dollars and many nights of stress because we overpaid for it.

Lucky for us, we'd hired a financial advisor when we got pregnant with our son, and had bought some life insurance policies. We made sure we were depositing savings in our 401K, and always had a small emergency fund set aside. Other than that, we didn't think about saving or why it mattered. Our decision-making process was that we'd "checked off the boxes." Besides that, we were on autopilot. I had no long-term savings goals in place.

By the time I was 31, I had a great savings account, thanks to my employer, yet I was also already $20K in credit card debt. Our house was $167,000 underwater because we had bought it in Las Vegas right before the financial bubble burst in 2008. We didn't know about investments, but I had the drive and the will to learn. One, I wanted to help other people because that is a passion of mine. Two, I knew I needed to help myself first.

## I decided to take a long hard look at my money.

# LEARN ABOUT MONEY

I became a financial advisor to learn about money, and teach myself about money. I was on a mission to teach myself about money so I could teach others. I wanted to achieve financial freedom, get out of debt and make my money on my own. I wanted to make a difference in this world—that has always been my mission at heart. I went into financial planning because I saw it as the opportunity for me to generate wealth, and make an impact on people and the planet. I knew that I could make it happen, and I had a lot of confidence in myself. So, I started working on socially responsible investing because I wanted to teach clients how to invest their money in a socially responsible way so they could also create and maintain wealth, and so they could invest with solid companies also doing their part in the world.

I worked really hard. Woke up early every day and went to bed late. I attended conferences, and surrounded myself with people in the finance industry. I worked with an elite team of wealth advisors who are all at the top of their game. I was determined to make it and I knew I had to invest in myself along the way. Of course, I was willing to do that.

We were pushing the pedal to metal trying to make something of ourselves, but my husband and I broke ourselves in the process.

We were exhausted. I was resentful because I didn't feel like my husband was pulling his weight while I was working full-time, and taking my son to and from daycare each day. My husband worked nights and we never saw each other. When we weren't working, we were trying to keep up with social functions and keep our house intact. Because we were so ragged, we took it out on each other. It was far from an "ideal" life.

So, I made the decision to quit my job and stay home. That's when all the shit came down. We went from two incomes to one.

My husband also started a new career in management. We took big risks all at once. As a result, we lost steady income, and my husband had to leave a couple of jobs. **Thankfully, we had some money saved, because there was no plan B but the savings.**

Then, in 2016, I decided to start my own company. I thought I could do it on my own because of everything I was going through. I was digging and creating, with the belief I could make it.

For three years, I thought I could build a business helping millionaires... but I found myself down to my last $20,000 dollars. My business was not where I had envisioned it would be when I first opened the doors.

I knew better, but I didn't know how to stop the bleeding. I wasn't willing to give up on my dream, so I kept plowing on. But I feared people would find out and judge me, and I feared losing everything. I'd made a commitment to not ask my parents for help... ever, and it seemed like I might have to do that. I was afraid I had made the wrong decision, and that I'd have to get a "real job." The fear that I didn't have what it took to be successful in the industry kept me up at night.

What I feared most was looking bad and failing. I never feared homelessness, but having my reputation damaged was like death to me. I was afraid that despite the successes I'd had over the years, failing at becoming a financial advisor was going to damage people's perceptions of me to the point I would never recover.

## MEET ANGIE

She also grew up never having money.

But she scheduled a call to speak with me after she saw one of my videos, "Stop spending money on stupid shit."

In Angie's words:

"I had no relationship with money, and at 16, I was still very naïve as to how to make money and save it. My mom was a single mom of three. We were always broke, and lived in low-income housing, using food stamps and whatever other help my mom received from the state. I was on my own at about 16 and half when I was placed in foster home for a short, short period. In that time, I owned nothing. I went to high school and worked at blockbuster. Then I started working in a restaurant where I made good money but always kept spending it. Everything changed when I became pregnant at 19. I still had no savings and no idea what to do with the little amount of money I'd made. For about 4-5 years, I was a single mom working in a daycare, and bringing my daughter to work before leaving for a waitress shift at night. I still never had enough."

When Angie got money, she spent it. She didn't keep track of it. She spent more at Target each month than she liked to admit, rather than making wise choices. She was trying to keep up with everyone else. She didn't know where to start nor did she feel confident in her ability to make it happen.

She knew she had money problems. At a certain point, it wasn't the scraping by that was the issue. When she got older, she made great money.

The problem wasn't her "earning," it was her "spending."

Angie is smart and talented. But "poor" was the only thing she'd ever known. According to Angie, on the inside, she didn't believe she was worthy of having money.

She was not managing her money well, but she has an intense desire to know more, and to do more with it. She just didn't know how.

Here's what I also learned about Angie.

Angie works harder than <u>anyone</u> I know.

She's a beautiful go-getter and has serious grit! Before I spoke with her, I thought she had it all together. But then she made an appointment with me and no-showed the first time. LOL—I thought, *she'll be back when she's ready*. The second time she scheduled a call, we got deep—fast.

Angie is a director of sales and catering of a large restaurant group in Las Vegas and a single mom to two daughters. She has worked hard through the ranks of the food and beverage industry. Angie knows how to create major financial results for her company having generated over $1.3 million in sales in a year and a half.

Deep inside, Angie was not happy. She was working 60 plus hours per week, and despite her appearance of having it all together was resentful and bitter. She knew she wasn't getting paid her worth and she desperately wanted out. Angie was committed when she hired me. She knew there had to be something bigger and better out there for her, she just didn't know where to start.

We started with her tracking her money. I teach my clients about their money types (that I have borrowed from my coach), and it was no surprise when Angie's test revealed she is a spendthrift money type. Basically, she loved spending money but often had guilt or shame after spending money, but she just couldn't stop! Within months of tracking her money and using the same methods I will teach you in this book, Angie was able to shift her behaviors and beliefs to more conservative spending and within months had shifted her money type into a new category—cheap! She laughed out loud when she took the test for the second time during our second weekend of the SISTER mentorship. She was really proud of the fact she had changed her spending habits in such a short period of time.

Here's what it took: Angie had to get serious about her money. She had to stop spending money and learn how to slow down her life. She had to learn how to save money for unforeseen circumstances, and she had to believe (even during the tough moments of life) that she was worthy of having money, and telling her money who was boss—rather than continuing to let money control her.

Not only has Angie turned her financial situation around, she has discovered her true passion in life. After working hard on aligning her purpose in life with the financial choices she was making, she realized that she wanted to help people. That was her driving force. Helping people like she had was when was younger, working with the elderly in an assisted living home was something that she longed to do. Her limiting belief she couldn't do that and make money and her lack of confidence with money stopped her from pursuing her real dream of helping from her heart.

# When she got clear about her money, she got clear about her life.

After a long conversation with her about a month ago she told me she dreams of owning an elderly care facility. She wants to be with elderly people. She wants to take care of them, to be their angel as they come to the end of their lives. Angie has a gift at giving back. When she talks about making a difference in this world, her entire face lights up and tears come to her eyes.

Angie's limiting beliefs about her self-worth and her inability to control her money have been holding her hostage her entire life. When I met her, she was someone who spent money frivolously on items that didn't matter to her; she was trying to keep up with the appearance of being successful. Only four months after working with me (and she sure was tested), she learned she is worthy and capable of having it all. She shifted her belief that she couldn't do it, or make it happen into using her voice and standing up for what she believes in.

Angie aligned with her personal belief that she can have what she wants, and she is worthy of having it. She decided she can make the amount of money she wants and that spending money on stupid shit isn't serving her life.

I remember my first conversation with Angie. She was frustrated and more than anything, was tired.

Me: "Angie, what are you frustrated about right now?"

Angie: "I'm frustrated that I know I make good money but I don't know where it goes each month! I want to have money in savings, and I'm tired of living paycheck to paycheck."

Me: "If you could change anything right now what would it be?"

Angie: "I want to know that I'm making the right choices with my money, but I don't know how to do that. I want to take a vacation. I don't want to feel bad about spending money. I need help."

Just a *simple shift* in her mindset has made a huge difference in her life. Since then, Angie has received a $10K raise, and a job offer that would pay her double what she's making now. She's healthier than she's been since she's had her kids. She's stashed over $5K in savings and has serious plans to go back to school and pursue her nursing degree and ultimately her dream of owning an elderly care home.

# MONEY BELIEFS

Money beliefs are those inner conversations that we have learned from others or have picked up subconsciously over time. Money beliefs develop as children when we watch our parents or parental figures handle (or mishandle) their money. They are the drivers in how you make decisions with your money moment-to-moment.

People develop their money beliefs out of a resentment or resistance to the way their parental figures were with money. For example, maybe they grew up broke; their family never had money. At one point, they decided NOT to be like that. They were tired of scraping by and believed that money was going to be the answer to their problems. Those beliefs drive their decisions (perhaps yours) today.

Money beliefs are developed over time by life experiences. Something happens to us and through that experience we decide who we're going to be about money, or what we think is a fact. When we work together, you learn what we think is a belief is just an opinion. This is an empowering money breakthrough and it is one Angie was excited to experience. Typically, money beliefs come from the past and through observing other people.

The <u>main</u> limiting money beliefs my clients have:

1. "I'm not worthy (of having what I want and having the wealth I desire)."
2. "Other people won't like me if I have money."
3. "If I have money, I'm greedy."
4. "I don't need money to be happy."
5. "I don't know what to do with my money or who to trust with it."

As women, we have different spending characteristics. Usually depending on how we're feeling. These characteristics are emphasized when we're feeling stressed, fearful or in scarcity. They also dictate how we behave with our money. Our spending characteristics reflect who we are about money (aka—our money beliefs) and they manifest through how we actually use our money. We can earn, save, invest, and spend. And everyone does these in different combinations. The combination of earning, saving, investing, and spending is what I call our <u>Money DNA</u>.

For example, have you ever said, "I work my ass off but I just can't seem to get ahead?" Meaning, you're earning money, and spending it (on bills, life, etc.) faster than it's coming in? Then, you want to jump into action and "fix it" so rather than having a balanced approach or a "have it all" approach, you shift everything into the SAVE category because you believe that's going to be the fix. Two months later, what happens? You feel broke. You are a slave to your job. You've got money in savings but you're miserable because you aren't spending it and you really, really want to go that concert next weekend. Sound familiar?

**Most people think that *spending* is bad, and *saving* is good. But that's not always true.**

What causes us the most pain is when spending and saving are disproportionate to the other. It's easy to feel like you're not balanced in your life when you're only concentrating on one of the above behaviors. Instead, you must have a balanced plan that is going to give you the ability to EARN, SAVE, and SPEND in harmony. I'll teach you more about this concept later in the book, but I want you to BELIEVE it's possible. Because it is possible. I have clients who are earning more, saving more, paying off debt and spending money and they are feeling free as they tackle their money obstacles. They followed my steps and are finally living again with the understanding that as their money behaviors move them forward at they can still truly enjoy their money. Wouldn't you like to enjoy your money? I know you just replied with a resounding "Yes!"... Who wouldn't want to get more out of their hard-earned cash?

It is important to know that your behaviors and beliefs about money aren't "bad" or "good." They are either working for or against you, and what's most important is that they are aligned with your purpose and goals in life. If your decisions aren't aligned with what you say you really want, you will work against what it is you say you want. I'll teach you some easy mindset changes and actions you can take and do as you read along in this book to understand if you're acting on purpose with your money or not. Here's a good one to start with.

# EXERCISE

## Your Money Beliefs

Here's what you should do next:

1. Write down a time you made a bad decision with your money where you felt really bad afterward (spent money on clothing you didn't need, spent money at Target on things you didn't need, made a major purchase out of emotion and put it on a credit card, and so on).

2. How, specifically, did you feel after you made this decision (guilt, shame, fear)? What reasons or justifications did you give yourself for making the decision?

3. Describe a time when you made a choice with your money that made you feel good. (E.g., you negotiated for a higher wage at work, or decided to finally pay off your credit card.)

4. How, specifically, did you feel after you made this decision (joy, contentment, accomplished)? What reasons or justifications did you give yourself for making this decision?

5. Reflecting on your answer for question number four, if you were faced with potentially making that same decision again, would you do the same thing or choose a different option? If so, what would you do, and why? How would that make you feel?

CHAPTER 2

# Your Driving Force

*"Whatever you choose, however many roads you travel, I hope that you choose not to be a lady. I hope you will find some way to break the rules and make a little trouble out there. And I also hope that you will choose to make some of that trouble on behalf of women."*
—Nora Ephron

## MEET SARAH

Here's a conversation we had when she first hired me.

>**ME:** Sarah, I'm going to ask you some questions, "What's important about money to you?"
>
>**Sarah:** Okay, got it.
>
>**ME:** Then, after you answer, I'm going to ask another question. Just trust it's going somewhere. There are no right or wrong answers, okay?
>
>**Sarah:** Okay, no problem.

**ME:** Alright, Sarah. What's important about money to you?

**Sarah:** What's important about money to me is that my bills are paid.

**ME:** Cool. Okay – What's important about your bills being paid?

**Sarah:** LOL—um. Well, if my bills are paid then I don't have to worry about it.

**ME:** What's important about not worrying about it to you?

**Sarah:** If I don't have to worry about my bills being paid then I can be more present for my kids.

**ME:** What's important about being present for your kids?

**Sarah:** Because I want them to know they are loved and that they matter.

**ME:** What's important about your kids knowing they are loved and that they matter to you?

**Sarah:** Sigh… I want them to have confidence.

**ME:** What's important about your kids having confidence?

**Sarah:** Because I'm working hard to be successful and I want them to be successful and good human beings

**Me:** What's important about your kids being successful and being good human beings?

**Sarah:** Duh… what else is there? LOL. Because they'll make the world better. I want to make the world better.

**Me:** What's important about making the world better?

**Sarah:** I want other women in the world to know they matter. I want them to have freedom and peace. That's what I want for me and I want that for them, too.

**Me:** What's important about having freedom and peace?

**Sarah:** (With tears in her eyes.) Because that's the life I want. I want to be peaceful and free to do what I want. I didn't have that as a kid, I didn't have confidence, and I want to be that and teach my kids how to do that, too.

**Me:** (Not knowing we reached her "why.") Sounds like an amazing world to me.

When it comes to money, every single time when I sit down with a client and talk about their driving force of their money, repeatedly, their first answer is rooted in the need to survive; to take care of their basic needs. Their response fits into the responses found on the bottom of Maslow's hierarchy of needs, a pyramid created from years of research to investigate what it takes for people to get to self-actualization. Our need to provide for our survival is uncomplicated and raw. When we work through our self-limiting money beliefs, we can move up the pyramid and think more critically about our money as well as give ourselves different beliefs and goals.

This concept is used in many organizational behavior environments where the organizations are looking at, *"How do we become a self-actualized organization? How do our clients become self-actualized?"*

This exercise is done in financial planning as well, where we ask the question, "What's important about money to you?" Of course, the first thing a person will say is, "Taking care of my basic needs."

Most people aren't clear about what's important to them in life and business. This is normal. Because most are stuck in survival. And when you are stuck in survival mode, just feeding yourself, having a place to live, and taking care of basic needs, you won't find the time to ask yourself simple yet powerful questions.

When I work with my clients, we start at basic needs. Then I ask them what's important about those needs. Eventually they move up to the level of self-actualization. Imagine a step ladder; they go up one rung; then they go up to the next one, and somewhere in the middle of that step, a light bulb goes on! What matters to them are their relationships, giving back to the world, a fulfilling relationship with God, and working in their sense of purpose, whatever that means to them.

A lot of women find freedom at the top, because we, women typically don't give ourselves permission to be free in any area of our life. In fact, there aren't many of us, as demonstrated by the number of women leaders out there in the world, who are financially free.

I have many clients in their late 30s and 40s now, who had children when they were young, and what's important to them is that they break the cycle of poverty and survival for their children, that they're the leading example of that goal.

It's not until they stretch themselves higher and higher through this simple questioning process, that they realize money is so much more than just survival, that there's a huge gap in their ability to see the truth and understand it.

It's important for women to answer the questions that can help them discover self-actualization. We spend a lot of time concerned about what's important to other people, and how we're perceived in the world. We spend a lot of time comparing our bodies, and ourselves, and it's a losing game. When someone takes time to think about, without comparison to others, what's important to them as it pertains to having meaning and purpose in life, they start to understand they have profound meaning and talent, and they do have gifts they can give back. *They start to look at their lives differently; they will own their life differently.* When they're in full ownership of their talents, wants, and desires, they give other women permission to also be that way.

In the big picture of things, it creates a culture of leaders and not followers, but it also creates women who do what's right. They stand up and they stop the pattern of drama. Because drama comes from ignorance and hate and the negative events that have happened in their life. They can stop that cycle and focus on what matters, not just to them, but to the rest of the world. It has been my experience that most women want to give back.

*Once you clarify your purpose, your driving force, you can't go backward.* It's hard to deny it. That's the first step. Once you put words around your why and what you want, it's a lot harder to ignore what you've identified and push it aside.

But it's even harder if you don't have the right support and are surrounded by a bunch of people who have been in the same cycle and the same pattern; it takes a lot of courage to stand up and make new choices in new directions.

Women are good at self-sabotage, because we want to be liked, and loved. But what if what we want is different from the norm, from what we are living in our own lives? Reaching our goals is going to be difficult without the right support. We struggle because we don't feel worthy, and so we have self-worth conversations with ourselves. That's why I wrote this book.

Why is it important to have a clear driving force and purpose in your life? Let's start with someone who's unclear or who doesn't know what they want. This classic person will come into my world having spent a ton of money on *stupid sh\*t (aka things that don't create sustained happiness in their lives).*

That's a person who will overspend in debt, who will lend money out to people. Because they don't have clarity or focus on where that money needs to go, they'll still give that money away, or they'll lend it to other people and maybe never ever get it back.

It may not even be that they have a problem creating wealth, it's that it's coming in and going out just as quickly. They feel less satisfied with their life, no matter how much stuff they have. If they have a house filled with amazing things—it could be Joe Schmo with a mansion but because he's got money and he's not clear on the direction of his life or why his money matters, he's just as miserable as someone who doesn't have money, or who's in a totally different financial situation—they still won't be able to fill their emotional void by buying stuff.

Additionally, they are probably not going to spend on things that are good for their well-being, and they might overspend on alcohol, tobacco or have a gym membership they never use. *They also are going to throw money at problems, to fix their problems.*

If you were to sit down and ask them, "Why did you spend your money on that?" they can't explain. There's no intention behind their actions. They're also unfortunately easily manipulated, so they could readily follow someone, and become a victim of a scam, because they're chasing the money rather than getting clear on what they want.

And if you offer a long-lasting solution, they might say, "I don't have the money for it..." But all their money is going somewhere else. Into solutions that *don't* work and are temporary. Such as drinking, overeating, and buying stupid sh\*t so they can fill a void.

They aren't bad people for doing it. It's just that no one has showed them what works, what doesn't, and how to get out of it. The first step is getting clear on your *driving force.*

In contrast, let's examine women who have a focused driving force; these are the women who walk into a room and they're noticed. But they don't stand out because they start drama. They don't bring attention to themselves. No, they're women who show up, and are perceived as having their sh*t together.

People who know what they want with their life are productive people. They're people who can speak well on what's important to them, women who wrap themselves around organizations or non-profits for causes that matter. They give, are generous of their time, are healthy in conversation and healthy physically. I mean, no one's perfect, but they take care of themselves.

They would be someone, if given an opportunity, who would be able to say, "Hey, let me think about that," and then they could make their decision based on: "Okay, is this something that's important to me, or is it not important to me? Am I going to invest in it? Am I not going to invest in it?" They're also women, unfortunately, who might get a bad name or a bad rap in business, so they could be perceived as the Alpha, because they are super clear about what they want and they're not going to take any bullshit. That is not always honored, not yet anyway, in our world.

I'll give you another example. When I met Danielle, she felt like a doormat in her relationships. Her real superpower is that she's a generosity rock star. She loves to give; she's built for it. She wants to give to people, to support people, and she's adopted three children. So, you can see it's just in her DNA to give, but her giving was so out of balance that she had completely lost herself and what was important to her in her life.

She was in a marriage that wasn't working, and had over $20,000 in credit card debt as well as no money in savings. The first several meetings, she was in tears, and asked "What am I doing with my life? How am I going to get out of this mess?" Her questions revolved around how she could fix what was wrong.

As we shared about the pain she was in, I kept saying to myself, *you're not alone. It's going to be okay. You just can't see it yet. I want to work with you. I want to help you. I know I can.*

Her life was working, though, I think it's important to note that. She has a stable job she loves. She's making over $80,000 a year. Her life wasn't in shambles, but she wasn't clear about the direction she was heading in her life, and she didn't have the confidence and clarity to make empowered choices with her money.

Does that sound familiar?

When I start working with a new client, I have them get clear on how bad their financial situation is and how bad it isn't, because we all think our financial situation is doomsday. It really doesn't matter how much debt we have. It's not the end of the world. *How we perceive our money will frame our reality.* The first thing that I shifted her perspective on was what the actual situation was, and how to take a breath.

She needed to do this so she could stop her fear, anxiety, and her habit of chastising herself about behaviors. I let her know she was going to be okay.

She was so hard on herself and so ashamed of her debt, feeling, *how did I get here?* She was embarrassed about the dynamic she had created with her husband, because she was supporting their family financially. More and more of us women are getting there in life, but it still doesn't feel great when we don't have a husband who's supporting us financially, even if they're our partner financially. The financial downward spiral along with many other aspects led to a diminishing relationship. She was lonely and quite resentful that she had let this situation develop in her relationship.

I offered her a refuge. We sat down, talked, and I gave her some perspective, let her know she wasn't alone, that she did have a partner, someone who was going to help her get out of the mud. Then we looked at her money and got clear on what she actually does have in her accounts, and what would be possible for her. We put a system in place that she could handle.

She has three beautiful children. What she wanted most was to buy a house and to be with her family. To do that, we needed to rebuild her credit and reduce her debt.

She just needed some course correction, and somebody to be a sounding board. I was like, "Yes, do this; no, don't do that. It's not worth your time." We put a debt repayment plan together, and she learned she could and can support herself financially. She realized a new, independent life was on the horizon and for the first time in a long time, was excited for her kids' future, but more importantly, she was excited for her future.

Her biggest hurdle was that she had all these little credit cards; a Victoria's Secret card for $300, a Kohl's card for $300, and a Bath and Body Works card for $200. She was using these cards because she wanted instant gratification, rather than understanding if she had the money to purchase new items or not. Ten credit cards with all these small balances were drowning her in monthly minimum balances. After our first meeting, she stopped using those credit cards completely.

Once she stopped using those credit cards, she started repaying them one at a time. She implemented the *snowball effect* of paying down debt, and got really clear about what she had to spend every month, and what she didn't have to spend every month. She gave herself a spending account. Now, she has two accounts; she spends out of one, and pays six bills out of the other. All my clients do this now.

After working with me for just six months, Danielle has paid off over $15,000 in debt, while finalizing her divorce and starting her new single life. If you ask her, she will tell you she's never been happier because she is finally living a life she knows she was meant to be living. Her money chaos is over. She's clear and confident about what decisions she makes with her money, and she is pursuing her passions using her driving force of giving to guide her. She has money in savings, is saving for travel, and is making travel plans to do the things she loves. When she cries these days, it's because she's happy, not because she's sad anymore. She beams when I see her, and she's confident. She's in control of her money, and now she's in control of her life.

I know you're asking yourself what you need to do to shift your life from financial stress and chaos to paying down debt, having money in savings, and making confident choices with your money. My clients come to me with the exact same questions. Before I teach you what to do with your money, you must first understand what is influencing your decisions about money. Is it scarcity and fear, or is it your driving force and purpose? This exercise will help you get clearer about your driving force. Once you get clear, it will be that much easier for you to make choices that serve your purpose, and get you on your unique path.

# **EXERCISE**

## Clarify Your Driving Force

Answer the following questions:

- What's important about money to you?
- When you are dead, what's going to matter the most about your life?
- What are people going to say about you, when you are gone?
- What do you want your children to say about you?
- What regrets would you have if you died tomorrow?
- What are the causes that matter to you?
- There's a lot going on in the world right now. What are the things that pull at your heart? If you could make a difference what would it be?
- What are the non-material things in your life that you value?
- What are five things that aren't working in your life right now? Next to each item, list how those things could be different.
- Take money off the table. If you could do any job what would it be?

CHAPTER 3

# Standing In The Gap

*"Transformation begins with the radical acceptance of what IS."*
—Danielle LaPorte

WHEN I MET EMILY, she had just left her job as a corporate trainer for a big athletic company that focused on Pilates, fitness, nutrition, etc. She knew she wanted to start a business. She knew she had the expertise to do it. But she had to be willing to take a leap into the unknown. She hired me because she knew she needed a mentor, someone to teach her how to start her business. Shortly after hiring me, she opened her doors.

But Emily didn't know how to run a business or how to brand herself. She had no idea what she was getting herself into. All she knew was that it was time for her to stop working for other people, and to try to make something for herself, on her own.

Emily hasn't always been good with money. Most of my clients have a history of making decisions that are not helping them financially. Similarly, Emily was struggling to make ends meet as a personal trainer, not because she wasn't awesome. She's incredibly talented! Emily has lived in financial scarcity her entire life. Even when times were great, she would sabotage her opportunities, because she wasn't used to having money. She didn't know what to do with it.

Here's the truth: most people are just like Emily. They have gotten so used to playing the game of financial "survival" that it's actually UNSAFE for them to win. Let me explain. Your brain wants to keep you safe and to do so it tells you if you're actually winning in life that you're not safe. You then snap back to the day-to-day game of keeping up with the paychecks. It's not your fault, and it wasn't Emily's either.

For Emily to be successful she had to be willing to stop looking at her past for answers. She had to be willing to stand in the gap between her past and her future. She had to accept she was in new territory, looking forward to her future, but that she still had a long way to go before she was there.

She has been standing in the gap ever since, and looking forward to what she wants to create.

We looked at her money behaviors, beliefs and values. She didn't grow up financially stable. At the age of 29, she took a stand for herself.

Emily joined my SISTER Mentorship and hit the ground running with her business. She learned how to charge her worth and most importantly, manage her money. In just four months, she generated over $10,000 in her first business. She's moving and making progress and signing new clients. She doesn't know from month-to-month where her paycheck is coming from, but she is doing it anyway.

What's different for Emily now is that she has the confidence and clarity of how to make money in her business. She has worked to remove toxic people from her life and surround herself with people who support her mission. Every day, she wakes ready to work and find ways to make her business succeed. When we first met, she knew she needed a mentor. Now, she never has thoughts of giving up even though she endures the ups and downs of life and business. She's on a mission to help the women she serves.

In this chapter, we talk about *standing in the gap*. But what specifically is the gap? The gap is the unknown. At some point, you must face forward and look to the future. Even in the process of gaining awareness, there must be a time where you can't look back any further. There are no more answers in the past. People get stuck looking to the past to make sense of why they do what they do. You must look forward, to design life, into the future.

We need to accept what works with us and what we want, and then we can look forward into our future, and build a vision for ourselves.

Financially, the gap means it is where we are we today, and where we want to go. Traditional advisors measure the GAP quantitatively. For most people, this is hard. If you ask people how much money they want to have by the time they are 55, if they say three million, they have no idea what it means to them today, or what they need to do in the shorter term to get there. This is why I focus my messages on non-financial advising.

You must gaze forward and start thinking about getting out of the hole. Determine to make moves with exact certainty or clarity on what your life is going to be like in 20 years. Standing in the gap means being COMFORTABLE with being UNCOMFORTABLE.

It means being comfortable with any anxiety, fear, or doubt that comes up. But it also means embracing the exhilaration and excitement that arises when you take actions toward what you truly want. There is hope!

# Standing in the gap is a sign things are changing. Because you are exploring new ground. And new ground feels uncomfortable.

You may be wondering, why is it important to stand in the gap? First, you are there in the gap anyway. If you are reading this book and have told yourself *I got to get my shit together*, you are not where you want to be exactly. You could lie down in the gap, stay there, or take a stand and start moving in any direction. But you must acknowledge there IS a gap.

Second, standing in the gap and taking action can lead to big transformation. If you keep making the same decisions you've made in the past, nothing is going to change going forward. A sign that you are doing the same things you did in the past is that it feels *comfortable*.

I'll give you an example. When I met Valerie, from the outside looking in, her life seemed problem-free. Valerie is stunning, tall and put together even in yoga pants. Her home is fully furnished and also beautiful. There is nothing wrong. She's not a mess. She makes over $100,000 a year. She was over $40,000 in debt. She wanted to get out of her relationship, but she didn't know how to manage her money. She wasn't confident or clear on what she was doing with her money and why. She was afraid of spending it. She had anxiety. When she spent money it felt good, but only in the moment.

When we went through a lot of the exercises to gain clarity on what she wants in her life, the first step she had to take was to accept, *"Okay I'm not where I want to be."* She acknowledged she wasn't living from purpose. She was not connected to her WHY. And she was waking up like a zombie and going to work every day where she could hit goals and make stuff happen even though she lacked confidence about the direction of her life. Not knowing what to do with her money scared her. A lot of the time, she would freeze when it came to making her money decisions because she was afraid she would make a wrong choice. After working with her for a few hours during our strategy session, many opportunities opened up for her. At that point, she could see she had been so busy chasing a paycheck she wasn't living a life she loved.

What she realized was she really loves giving. She loves being a healer. She loves supporting other people. She accepts herself as a leader. She is a center of influence for her friends and family. She decided her relationship wouldn't control her.

When she joined the SISTER mentorship, she was in the gap of not having those things but wanting them. And not knowing how to go about getting them. But within four months, her entire life shifted: she started a new meaningful relationship, and crushed her sales goals by over $700,000 this year. Now, she is stepping into leadership at work, and she just bought a house.

Here's the thing, though: the gap never goes away. You don't reach a point where you have closed the gap.

## Standing in the gap is what gives you power

But your position of power is only relevant if you act. You must feel uncomfortable, and take action anyway. I stood in the gap when I said, "This is going to happen" and "I can build a business that will make a difference." Those were my thoughts when I left my company and started my own business. The biggest gap for me was seeing what was possible:

- Get out of debt.

- Build a sustainable model.
- Help people.

I then noticed how far off I was from my goals. But looking into my future, I knew I could make a difference. I knew I was going to have a successful business helping women. I could see, taste, and touch the vision I had in my head of being in front of a room of inspiring women, challenging the status quo. When I looked at my current life and the life I aspired to, I could see the gap was great. I was broke, had no clients and no branding. My business and I were at square one. My typical past excuses for why I couldn't be successful, why I couldn't take a trip I wanted, and why I couldn't buy an item I wanted was that I didn't have money. When I started my business, this limiting belief of "not enough" showed up over and over again. Rather than giving it power or letting it stop me, I had to be willing to take a risk, and make money in my business even though I had just spent my last $20,000 to invest into my coach.

I wasn't seeing the bigger picture. Instead, I placed all my attention on how there was not enough money to do what I wanted.

Today, when I get stuck, I act anyway—even if I don't know where the money is going to come from, even if I'm afraid, even if I am not feeling confident. The only way for me to thrive is to take action despite how I feel. I may not feel like doing what I need to do, but I keep going forward. Rather than being in that conversation for too long, like 20 minutes, I ask myself "Well, what's next? What do I need? What do I want?"

That's why, back when I was building my business, I wrote financial goals for myself every month.

- Jan - $4,000
- Feb - $6,000

- March - $8,000.

I declared I would make $4,000 in the first month. On Jan. 15, I was a bit behind. I needed to make $1,500 more to reach my goal, to move forward, and take the next step. I called my coach, and said, "I need two more clients to make this happen." Then, I focused on closing those two clients and got back on track. I took the right action.

For me, it means that every single day, I don't know what the next day will hold. Someone asked me, "How do you do it?" I replied, "I don't know day-to-day if this is going to work but I wake up and do it every day."

One of my favorite things to do in the morning is to take a walk with my dog. There are mornings where I don't feel happy. I feel lost. I'm not sure what my focus for the day is going to be. Some days, I wake up worrying about a number of things, making money, paying off debt, my son's health, my health, etc. Women are really great at worrying—about everything!

My morning walks help me connect and get present with nature, and with God. I take the time I need to practice gratitude, I listen to meditations (Abraham Hicks is currently my go-to). The one mindset hack that gets me back into action and shifts my perspective when I notice that I'm coming from scarcity and fear rather than abundance and joy is I will ask myself, "Do I have everything I need today?" Every day, the answer is YES. I have a home to live in; my bills are paid; I have clothes to wear. When I recount these blessings, my doomsday attitude shifts, and I realize my life is not going to fall apart that day. There is food in my fridge, and I can be free to focus on what I need to focus on to help my clients and keep going.

The gap is standing in the belief and the vision it is going to happen. There is uncertainty. I am comfortable with being uncomfortable. I am certain in my vision, and I trust myself. I trust that what I want for other people and how I want to help other people, is valuable, and that it matters. I just wake up every day figuring it out, how to make my business and service more impactful etc.

The same goes for my clients. There will be times you feel stuck. But the important thing is to stand in the gap and find a way to take action anyway. Even if that means getting help. I'll give you an example: Charlene. When it gets hard, she stops. She avoids. She avoids with food.

In Charlene's words: "I avoid by eating out in rich, over-the-top experiences and hanging out with other people. Those experiences help me avoid the fear that resides when I think of what I'm going to have to do to accomplish my dreams. Unknowingly, I was turning my back, even if momentarily, on my dreams because I was avoiding owning up to my dreams."

Charlene avoids by hanging with other people, are you avoiding? How do you avoid?

Charlene has a big vision for her life, but when things get scary and uncertain, she bails, I won't hear from her for a while.

When people don't know what to do, I tell them, "First and foremost, acknowledge you are stuck. Then pick up the phone and ask for help."

That's why coaching is so valuable. As a coach, I can help people figure-out what stuff got them stuck; I can ask questions to clarify, and give them perspective.

When Charlene first got stuck it would be for two or three weeks, but we had an agreement. We always have calls together, and she would always show up even if she wasn't executing anything. Even when she was stuck. She would go out after one meeting, understanding the agreed-upon actions, and nothing would get done. But that doesn't mean it wouldn't happen. Women committed to transforming their lives, and businesses, and money—must stick with it. Stay committed even if you get stuck.

Charlene, kept asking: "WHY do I need to do this?" From a coaching perspective, the WHY doesn't matter. That's looking back at the past. At a certain point, we must choose the path of what it is and stop looking back for answers. We must stand in the gap and look forward.

Now, I'm a money coach. I'm not a money therapist. So, I said, "WHY will keep you stuck. The most important questions are, "What do you want?" and "What are you committed to?" A light went off for Charlene when she heard me say that. She knew that I wasn't going to let her use her past as an excuse for not getting things accomplished any longer. Charlene realized she was afraid of commitment. She was asking WHY and that kept her in the same cycle of non-action. When we pushed forward and focused on what she wanted, and how she was going to make a difference, it shifted her. She got stuck a few times, and the more she looked forward and stopped asking why, the less time she spent in stuck-ness.

A financial advisor can give you a plan, but if you have no support implementing the plan, you are screwed. If life throws you a curveball, you don't know how to deal with it. When that happens, the first thing you must do is *gain awareness*.

One client was working hard to get herself out of the hole she had dug. She had $400 worth of transactions go through in her bank account. She didn't freak out. We stopped, looked at what happened, and identified how we could course correct. She talked to the bank, got the NSF charges refunded, and identified how much money she needed to get by before her next paycheck. She made that happen.

Planning is important. But having support to course correct is important, too. It will happen. Some days you just feel like crying. I will think *I'm crazy to believe I can actually do this. I'm crazy to think*

*I can have everything I want.* I will feel like crying because some days are rough and it can feel as if the fear of failure will get the best of me. Other days, I feel like crying because I'm overwhelmed, in a good way. My days are jam-packed with client meetings, interviews, and soccer games, and I get home exhausted. All I want is a glass of wine and to crawl into bed, but there's dinner to make. My son wants to read books. My dog is running around like a maniac, and these are all good things, but they are exhausting. Some days, I just need to know I'm not alone, and you do, too. Having a great network of other women to offer support to and to receive support from on those days really makes a difference, at least, it does for me. That's what the sisters are there for, to let you know: "You are not alone."

I want to invite you to be brave enough, to start looking forward into the future. There are reasons we don't do what we want to do. You must accept that you aren't where you want to be. Then start asking questions about what you really want in your life. Once you have answered those questions, you can take actions forward even if they scare you. That's standing in the gap.

# EXERCISE

## Stand In The Gap

It's hard to know what gap you're standing in if you can't clearly define it. With money, it's much easier to quantify how large the gap really is. The point of this exercise is for you to clearly begin to identify your financial gap. Your financial gap is that distance between where you are now and where you want to be when you hit certain goals in your life.

For example, one of the most important first financial goals you can set is to have an emergency reserve fund in place. Most of my clients set a goal to have at least one month's worth of income set aside, but ideally, it's 3-6 months. What do you make per month? Do you have that much in savings today? If not, what's the gap (aka the difference between what you have in savings and what you need to have in order to meet your emergency reserve goal)?

| | |
|---|---|
| One Month Income | $5,000 |
| Savings | $2,000 |
| Gap | $3,000 ($,5000 - $2,000) |

Financial gaps are much easier to determine than other gaps in your life. The following is a great example of how to quantify the gap so you can set measurable and achievable financial goals (my SISTERS call them S&M goals, lol!)

# QUANTIFY THE GAP

**Step One:** Identify one goal you have within the next 6 months that takes money to meet. (Aka travel to Costa Rica, have at least one month's worth of income emergency savings in place, pay off $5,000 in debt, remodel the kitchen, buy my first house.)

**Step Two:** Write down how much money you will need to meet that goal (goal total).

**Step Three:** Identify how much you have saved toward this goal (amount saved).

**Step Four:** Subtract Amount Saved from the Goal Total. The total is your gap.

What do the results tell you?

1. Notice the gap between where you are now and where you want to be.

2. Take a moment to check in with your physical sensations and thoughts.

    How do you feel about being in this gap? Does it excite you, or do you feel overwhelmed?

    Ask yourself how you're going to meet this goal, are you confused about where to start? Do you want to quit before you start? Are you telling yourself it's not possible, and that it won't happen?

    Or, are you ready to tackle this task, and do what it will take to meet that goal?

These are great examples of the thoughts and feelings associated with being in the gap. You know where you are; you know where you're heading, and the gap is the feeling and discomfort that comes from realizing you have work to do. The difference between a successful and unsuccessful person is the successful person decided she was going to stand in the gap and never give up on her goals. The unsuccessful person believed they were never going to reach their goals and gave up.

If you're ready to do whatever it takes to reach your goals in life, then you must be willing to get comfortable with being in the gap of where you are today and where you want to be. If you are unable to clearly define the gap, you will likely be off-target with your goals. Clearly defining the gap is an important part of meeting and exceeding financial goals.

# PART II.
# ACCEPTANCE

CHAPTER 4

# Your Hidden Superpowers

*"Everybody is a genius. But if you judge a fish by its ability to climb a tree, it will live its whole life believing that it is stupid."*
—Albert Einstein

YOU HAVE SUPERPOWERS. Whether you are aware of them or not. They are *monumental* to your capacity to make more money. In this chapter, we are going to clarify your superpowers.

Everybody is good at something. Even the kid with Down Syndrome can be good at making Starbucks coffee, being with people, and being joyful. I love that movie, *I Am Sam* (with Sean Penn). He showed up, did something he loved, and found purpose in it. In this process and through finding your purpose, it is unavoidable. There is no way to enjoy your life if you aren't doing what you love.

When I was an academic advisor for honors students, I worked with high-functioning brains. These were students who were geniuses and hard workers, people who learned how to be successful at whatever they put their minds to. I worked with students who scored perfectly on their SATs and ACTs and already thought that because they were good at certain subjects they were destined to go into specific fields. For example, students who excelled in math and science thought their only choice was to be an engineer or doctor. I watched many students go down that path. Some would to thrive. Others hated their lives. They failed at engineering, even though they had the mental capacity to be engineers.

Why? Their heart wasn't in it. They didn't like engineering. They had no idea or perception of what they could be successful doing other than being in a field where they could use their talent for math or science. Maybe they were great musicians but were limited in their beliefs that they couldn't be financially successful as musicians. Maybe they wanted to be architects but didn't realize they could change their trajectory and be happier. There are a lot of reasons why people don't follow their passions. For many, unfortunately, it's their perception they won't make any money doing what they love, so they settle for a career path they are less passionate about.

## People will pay you for your superpowers. Not for your misery.

You must understand your superpowers are not just your talents. It is where talent meets what you love. Where what you are good at also happens to be what you love.

We discover our superpowers by acknowledging and auditing what we excel at in our lives and businesses. We must audit our skills and take a long hard look at what we love to do and acknowledge what we don't love. Your superpowers are those activities and behaviors you simultaneously are great at and equally find pleasure in doing. Just because I developed a skill, I may not like doing it; that's not a superpower.

You also don't always have to do something well at first. You can hone things. For instance, I have not always been a great public speaker, but I love doing it, and I have gotten better at it over time. Sometimes, our superpowers need time to develop. But because they are our superpowers, when we give them attention and we apply ourselves in those areas, our growth becomes phenomenal.

The priority is to make sure whatever you choose to do gives you joy. Let me give you an example. Remember Sarah from a previous chapter? Sarah is a stay-at-home mom, and she has been selling Mary Kay Cosmetics. She joined the SISTER Mentorship because she wanted more out of life, and she knew she had to surround herself with people who propelled her. She thought Mary Kay was her answer. She'd had some success, but was not where she wanted to be.

She is creative, outgoing, and people focused. Those were the reasons she chose Mary Kay. However, it wasn't a fit because she didn't LOVE selling makeup. The keyword here is LOVE.

She didn't love selling makeup or products. It didn't give her excitement or joy. Her highest value was being a MENTOR and SUPPORT for women. So, she wasn't using her superpowers. She was caught up in selling makeup instead.

I asked Sarah, "What do people come to you for?" The answer to that question is a really good way to see what people identify as your value. She said, "Well, at church people always come to me when there is chaos and they don't know what to do." She's a critical thinker and great at troubleshooting and coordinating. Again, she loved Mary Kay for that. Her natural talents were:

- Being a critical thinker
- Troubleshooting
- Coordinating people

She always inspires people. She helps people feel calm in the storm. Together, we helped her get involved in a *new* business. Today, she is selling on behalf of a clothing company because the product is something she believes in and enjoys selling. As a result, she's made more sales in weeks than she'd made for years in Mary Kay!

I knew as soon as Sarah's newfound knowledge of who she was and what she loved doing clicked, she was going to see results fast. She finally had found the courage to make a change in her life and I was so relieved and grateful to know that and to see her head off in a new direction, so suitable to her superpower.

## HOW TO IDENTIFY YOUR SUPERPOWERS

So, how do you identify your superpowers? I'll share a quick exercise in a few pages. But the best way to start this journey, is to be courageous enough to get feedback from people. It scares the living daylights out of people to do this. And I get that it is scary. But, we can't always see for ourselves what's working and not working in our lives... it is too close to us. This is exactly why people can't understand their own money problems, especially women! There is not a large enough distance away from our emotions and our lives to form an objective opinion. I have clients who are financial accountants who can't manage their own money.

People watch you whether you realize it or not. And people are good, people CARE about you; they have thoughts about what works, what they love about you, and about what they feel are your talents.

If you are courageous enough, call 10 people you love and that you have 10 relationships with; get honest feedback on what your superpowers are in their eyes. If you don't have those kind of resources, take three people that you trust, who you know have your best interests, and ask them what they think your superpowers are. You might be surprised at the answers you get!

Here are signs that something is likely a superpower for you:

- You enjoy it.
- You don't have to work hard at it and you get a lot done.
- It doesn't *feel* like work.
- You lose track of time when you are doing it.
- Other people acknowledge you for it, even if you don't consider it anything special.

Here are some signs that something is likely not a superpower for you:

- You do work hard but get little return.
- You get exhausted and lose energy and motivation very quickly.
- You look at your watch or a clock and can't wait for the activity to be over.

When we are not using superpowers, we are going to experience more resistance.

# EXERCISE

## Superpower X-Ray

Set a timer for two minutes for each question, then write your responses. This activity is not something you want to overthink.

1. List all the things you have loved in your life.
2. List all the things you haven't loved in your life.

A lot of times what I do with women, is look back at what they have done with their money or careers, and identify what they don't want to do anymore. It makes them say, "I hate this shit!" Then I say, "Let's shift focus. What do you love and what are you good at?"

Now, I want you to look at your resume. Look at your work history throughout your life, at the organizations you have joined. Answer this question: What is the common thread?

I have always chosen jobs and experiences where I was working one-on-one with people. I was always an advisor, coach, mentor, or filling a role in that capacity. I was always advising people. When I reviewed my resume, I could see I gravitated toward it. I get people results. This is my superpower.

CHAPTER 5

# #Visioneering

---

*"Money is like the car you drive, it gets you places."*
—Lisa Chastain

VISIONEERING is being the person you want to be in the world. Then you develop a vision and a plan to get there. When I ask this question of my clients, I say, "Well, *who* do you want to be?"

Traditional goal setting in terms of money is often about setting a specific financial number. However, that's *not* visioneering. The money is just a *means* to an outcome. And there's the trap.

People get stuck on the *having* part of the vision. For example, having a house, the kids, a dog, a sports car, etc. There's nothing wrong with having things. But most people think that if they have those things, it'll make them happy. So, they spend their entire lives going for those types of possessions. The problem is once you do have those items, you aren't happy anymore. It's not sustainable.

In this chapter, I'm going to save you from the "goal" trap. It starts with knowing *who* you want to BE in the world. When you were a kid, you were asked, "What do you want to DO when you grow up?" versus "Who do you want to BE when you grow up?" We spend time on the wrong question.

I always thought I wanted to be a nurse or a teacher when I grew up. *Why*? I didn't know there was any other option for women. My mom was a stay-at-home parent. The only professions I saw women working in were in health-related and school-related fields. I had no idea what other women did for work in the world. I didn't think about who I wanted to be, whether a healer, a leader or visionary. These are not conversations many people have when they are young.

When you say: "I want to be joyful, compassionate, a great mother," etc., these are purposeful aims. That's who you are going to BE. Then, you are going to do things and plan things in alignment with your response. As a result of the things you do that are in alignment with your response, you will have the things you want such as; the income to invest in your BE-ing.

## BE-DO-HAVE

I stopped chasing stupid sh*t (aka objects that didn't feed my soul, or that cost a lot but gave me little satisfaction—like the Rolex watch I charged on my credit card and am probably still paying off 10 years later). My defining moment came when I was sitting on the couch one day when I was a stay-at-home mom. I had left my first career, and it was one in the afternoon. I drank wine as my, at-that-time three-year-old son was napping. My day was defined by his nap, and I would think *I can't wait till he naps so I can have a glass of wine.*

*Oprah* and *Ellen were on.* I still look up to those women because they are out in the world being amazing, helping, and interviewing people. The episode I was glued to was "Super Soul Sunday." Oprah was interviewing an expert on happiness from the Happiness University. I had to look inward and ask myself what was really driving my happiness as I watched and drank. I thought, *this is not what I had in mind for my life. Spaced out on the couch being a stay-at-home-mom. I'm wasting time and am completely disconnected from the woman I aspired to be in the world.*

As I reflected on the 5-year-old little girl that was me so many years ago, I was curious about what she would say to the mess of me on the couch that afternoon. I hated my life. I was going nowhere. I was stuck. That inner 5-year-old would have been screaming at me, **"Get off the couch!"** Sobbing, I knew my life was falling apart because I was chasing HAVING sh*t, a marriage, filling the house with furniture, and putting money in my bank account, I wasn't BEING who I was meant to BE.

**I wasn't living a life that aligned with my superpowers.**

I had to look at WHO I wanted to be. I wanted to be a LEADER, INSPIRING, COMPASSIONATE, a GIVER in the COMMUNITY. I wanted to be INTELLIGENT. That was my wake-up call.

# THIS IS YOUR WAKE-UP CALL.

A clearly-defined vision consists of all the plans in your life that have not yet come to fruition. If you found out you were going to die, you would immediately regret not taking your dream vacation, building your dream home, packing up in an RV and traveling cross country, having your first, second or third child, marry the man or woman of your dreams, starting that non-profit, and hugging your mom one last time. These are the moments and memories in life we work so hard to have. Unfortunately, many of us get so caught up in the hustle of life that we don't get to live out our dreams. I meet with clients who dream of traveling around the world, or who have been planning one dream trip for 10 years but have not taken it because life gets in the way.

The money is just feedback for what is working or what is NOT working in your life.

In my SISTER Mentorship, we do an exercise, and a light bulb goes off every single time we do it! Because the "doing-ness" and the "having" are just by products.

I'll give you an example: Loni wants to be responsible, so she can make more money for herself. But she's never lived her life more than a day at a time. She's never thought of her money as more than what she's had that day, or didn't have that day. This is not congruent. Because she wants to BE responsible. She wants to have a great new career. Ultimately, reaching both of those goals will give her the freedom to see her kids.

The truth is, Loni can't have any of that unless she commits to BEING responsible with her life, money, and her career. That's who she must be. So, when we talk about BEING-ness, it is more about a STANCE in your life. She wakes up every day to BE responsible. It is a choice.

Now, you can commit to three WAYS OF BEING in your life. For example, you can be compassionate, loving, etc. From there, ask yourself, what would a compassionate and loving person do? Match the activity to who you want to be. Then, you can make empowered choices. You will be in control about your choices, your life, and your money. The disconnect happens when you aren't connected to who you want to be.

When it comes to creating a vision with money, remember money's like the car you drive. It gets you places. So, using the BE-DO-HAVE paradigm as an example, I am committed to being a leader and I'm committed to being a business owner, so I can coach and mentor (the "doing" part of my career) women to have the life they want. Then my business financially will grow because, ultimately, I do want to be financially free meaning that eventually I would like to travel the world teaching women how to start their own businesses. I want to be a leader who helps women worldwide get out of poverty. My vision is filled with doing things that help women everywhere, and it has to start with my commitment to who I'm going to be in the world. From my actions, the doing follows. Not the other way around.

My vision for who I want to be in the world and who I'm working every day to be is generous, compassionate, and thought-provoking as a woman leader. My bigger broader vision of doing is connected to traveling the world teaching, mentoring, inspiring, and empowering women everywhere.

To do that I have to have financial resources. My life must work. My bills must get paid. I cannot be in debt trying to pay down debt. I must be able to freely hire somebody in my business and have the money to do that, so then I can go live a bigger version of myself. The money is so important and it's such feedback; I use it to ask myself: *is my business thriving or is it not thriving? Is my life thriving or is it not thriving?*

I don't mean I need a Ferrari. I don't care about that shit, but it's more like *can I afford my lifestyle? Can I afford the support I need, so I can be the woman I want to be in this world?* I know a lot of women are asking themselves these questions right now. As women, they hit home, don't they? That's why the money matters.

# EXERCISE

## Visioneering

Here's the exercise, construct a vision board with the following as a guide:

| BE #1 | BE #2 | BE #3 | BE #4 |
|-------|-------|-------|-------|
| DO    | DO:   | DO    | DO:   |
| HAVE  | HAVE  | HAVE  | HAVE  |

- There are four ways of being at the top. Under each way of being, you have a row for what you will DO, and what you will HAVE as a result of being that person.
- Place photos in each of the boxes that represent who you are being, what you are doing, and what you are having as a result.
- Place your vision board in a place where you can see it every day.

## CHAPTER 6
# Dealing With The #Haters

---

*"It is not the critic who counts; not the man who points out how the strong man stumbles, or where the doer of deeds could have done them better. The credit belongs to the man who is actually in the arena, whose face is marred by dust and sweat and blood; who strives valiantly; who errs, who comes short again and again, because there is no effort without error and shortcoming; but who does actually strive to do the deeds; who knows great enthusiasms, the great devotions; who spends himself in a worthy cause; who at the best knows in the end the triumph of high achievement, and who at the worst, if he fails, at least fails while daring greatly, so that his place shall never be with those cold and timid souls who neither know victory nor defeat."*
—Theodore Roosevelt

HATE IS A STRONG WORD. And I'm not saying that people are going to hate you. But when you make big changes, many people are going to be uncomfortable or feel challenged. Because suddenly who you are being in the world is going to change. For a lot of people, these changes can feel confrontational because you are detaching from the vision that *other* people have for your life.

**HATING
ANYONE
THAT
EXPERIENCES
RISING
SUCCESS**

We run into trouble because many of us want to please people. We want people to like us. But don't forget, the approval game is impossible because you are trying to win the approval of others or you want other people to see you in a certain way. You can't wake up and try to please 30 people because they all have different perceptions of you. It's impossible to win.

You must be willing to step outside your comfort zone and commit to who you want to be. That's what I mean by dealing with the haters. You must be brave.

At a very young age, I was going to be someone different than my dad wanted me to be. Now looking back, it was very clear. It wasn't so clear growing up. No, it was quite painful.

My dad's vision is and always has been family. Family's number one. What that means is that we spend every holiday together. We spend every birthday together. We do the same things together. He's the patriarch. Starting young, my first memory of this was in fourth grade. I was in gymnastics and I am a traveler. I love to travel. I am, and I was being independent. I wanted to go to a conference in Palm Springs when I was only about 10, My dad said, "No, you can't go. That's just not what we do as a family." I said, "I'm going anyway."

I did that repeatedly in my relationship with my family. Another time I wanted to go to a speed skating meet in Texas. I was 12 years old. It was Thanksgiving weekend. In my young life, I wanted to be ambitious, to be an athlete, and go for it, to travel from Vegas to Texas, and my dad said, not just "No!" but "Hell no. That's not who we are as a family. You need to be here for Thanksgiving." *I went anyway.*

As I remember it, I was really frustrated. I was sad and upset that he wouldn't let me go. I felt unheard and unsupported. I knew that being with my family was important and it put me in the position where I had to choose my family over this important trip. At such a young age, I had a fire in my belly to travel and experience the world, and I was willing to do that no matter the cost. Reflecting on that memory, I know this is who I still am today in the world. I push boundaries and limits in relationships; sometimes my decisions cause friction and hurt. Still, I strive to pursue my passions. This will never change.

A good result came from that situation. My dad loves me. My dad wants me with him. My dad wants me at holidays. I've missed a lot of family functions, but the feedback is that people noticed when I was gone; they hear me, and they love me. When I go to a family function, I will be peaceful with them because that's who I'm committed to being in the world. I'm not there to make them wrong for their choices.

## It's not that people don't love you. It's just that their vision for your life may be different from yours.

The other thing is that the clearer the vision, the clearer the voice. But yes, there will be people who disagree. So, the good feedback is people noticed, they heard and they wanted to be part of that conversation. They don't have to agree.

In my business, when people start showing up saying, "I don't agree with you," I know I'm onto something. I'm busting through a barrier. It's invigorating to know that I'm going to follow my gut and my instinct about what I want. The other advantage is that I'm proving to myself I can do it no matter who is in my life.

So, how do you deal with haters? First, realize no one is a hater. Hate is a strong word. Remember, people have a different vision for your life than you do. The next thing is, you deal with haters with compassion and love.

For example, if someone disagrees with you, you can ask yourself the following questions.

- Am I going to be confident? Yes.
- Am I going to be brave? Yes.
- Am I going to be compassionate? Yes.
- Am I going to be a leader? Yes.

Commit to who you are being. Now, when you are doing so, there are a couple of things that can happen. People in your life could say:

- "Yes, I'm in alignment with that."

Or…

- "No, no, no. That wasn't the plan. That's not who I want to be with you."

In the latter example, you could have a best friend who you've always done stuff together with only to wake up one day and say, "Hey, I'm going to be responsible with my money. I can't go to that concert," or "I can't go on that trip." Suddenly, your best friend's giving you shit and not supporting you. That happens. All. The. Time.

When you do get resistance, you must have a difficult conversation with that person. Especially if they are close to you. This person could also be your husband, life partner or work colleague.

# Being compassionate doesn't mean being a doormat.

You don't have to fight. The first thing you need to remember is that it's not personal. So, you have to tell the other person (the worst breakup line ever!): "It's not you. It's me."

Or you can say "I'm evaluating things and I'm thinking about what I want and it has nothing to do with you. It's not you. It's me."

From there, you must also be willing to say what you want. (Women have such a hard time with this, but we need to do it anyway.) That's why the visioneering process is so important because if we aren't clear with who we are being, we sure as hell can't tell somebody else what we want.

When we don't take this responsibility, we can get lost for decades in our lives because we aren't willing to stand up and communicate what we want. You've got to be willing to do that. Then you can enroll your haters to become supporters.

When I started out in the industry as a financial advisor in 2014, I went into business with my childhood best friend of 25 years.

We've always loved spending time together. We've always had a blast together. We love each other. She was my skating partner from my roller skating days. We traveled to meets and practiced together. I always hitched a ride because she'd gotten her license before me. In many ways, she was like a big sister.

Then she became my financial advisor. I thought I knew what she did, and I wanted to be financially successful. I wanted to be an advisor, too. Because I also wanted to help people. Everything aligned with who I wanted to be and what I wanted, with my compassion for other people. It all matched up with my desire to be socially responsible with investing.

She and her company told me they totally supported me. That was cool. I didn't have any experience and it was a brand-new field. It took a lot longer to work up the ranks than I thought, and it was a lot harder working for the firm than I'd imagined. Even though I was working with my best friend.

After three years, I realized we didn't work well together. Who we were being together and what we wanted ultimately, wasn't a fit. I got frustrated. My financial results were feedback that it wasn't working. I had blown through over $80,000 trying to make it work. I wasn't making any money, instead, I was actually $300 in the hole every month because my overhead was higher than my income. It sucked. It really, really sucked.

In that business partnership, trying to support myself financially, trying to support a business, trying to get clients, trying to support her business, it just wasn't evening out. So, I had to be willing to be honest with her.

She didn't agree with what I was doing, so, "hater," right? A very compassionate, loving hater. She was not on the same page with me and I was not on the same page with her. This example illustrates that when we use that word, it's really in the context of conflict.

The conflict was simply that her vision for the relationship was different than my vision for the relationship. I thought I was going into a full partnership. I thought I had complete say-so and I that I was going to be at the table making decisions. That wasn't the case, but I didn't know that.

It's not like she was bashing me or being horrible or dramatic. It doesn't have to be political. In the relationship, we were not a fit. I had to realize it wasn't working and I had to go into a conversation with her knowing I was ending the business partnership. This meant I had to have the courage to speak my truth because I knew that we didn't work well together, and she knew it, too. What I wanted, and what she needed, wasn't compatible. It was vital to stand in my truth of being compassionate and loving. I could've at any moment been horrible and been a victim to it all, but I had to take responsibility.

That's really important.

Things have changed between us, but there is still a lot of love. We have moved in different directions professionally, but I will always be grateful for the love and kindness she gave me throughout the years. She was my maid of honor for my wedding and planned my baby shower. Although this experience changed the dynamic of our relationship, we both learned a great deal about who we are in business and as friends. I will always love her, and am stronger because of her. Today she's got a thriving business in California, and my business is also thriving. I believe we taught each other so much.

## You must be willing to take full responsibility for what you've created in your life up until now.

You can't point the finger. There are extreme situations such as violence and abuse that don't fit here. But if you're in a job you hate, if you're in a relationship you hate, you have to own up to it. Have the courage to say, "This is not what I want. This is my vision. I'm going to go in a new direction."

When it comes to money, couples refuse to take responsibility all the time. When they're not clear going in about who's going to be responsible for what and who's making the decisions, it's confusing and communication greatly suffers.

# EXERCISE

## Silencing The Outside Voices

Who are the people in your life who have an influence over the decisions you make? Do you know which ones influences you positively or negatively? When it comes to making important decisions, do you know how to tap into your intuition and listen to yourself? Many of my clients struggle knowing how to listen to their own voices first. Self-trust is an important part of #adulting. If you can't trust your own voice to make decisions, you are likely spending time listening to people in your life who may love you but are not objective enough to help you make important decisions for what YOU want.

My clients typically struggle with feeling confident about their choices in life. Some of them spend a lot of time evoking answers from other people, their loved ones, significant others, and reading books from experts. The analysis of so many options often leaves them confused and stagnant. As soon as I can work with them to tap into their own wants, needs, and intuition, they begin to make decisions in their own best interest and guess what? Then they are happier than they've ever been because they are finally listening to themselves and learning to thrive on their own! Don't you want that? Aren't you ready to start living your own life free from others' opinions?

Making decisions on your own, accepting responsibility for the outcomes, and learning how to trust yourself are important steps in learning to listen to the voice within and silencing the outside voices. It is imperative that you learn how to do this, especially when it comes to making important decisions with your money. You can't make important decisions with your money if you aren't tapped into your own intuition, vision, and purpose for your life. Whose voice(s) are you really listening to?

Answer the following questions:

1. Who are the top three people in my life I call for advice?

2. How do I feel after I ask for advice from _____? (Do this for each person listed in question one.) Do I typically follow the advice of the people listed in question one?

3. Are the people above living the same life and lifestyle that I desire?

4. Who are the people in my life who are most negative about the decisions I make? (These people make me feel bad, make me doubt myself, make me angry.)

5. When I have an important decision to make, how often do I seek others for advice?

6. How often do I feel frustrated or confused by the advice offered by others?

7. When I listen to myself, and make decisions without others' opinions, how does it turn out?

After reflecting on your answers for each of the questions above, who do you believe in your life is most qualified to make important decisions for you?

My hope is that you have answered back with... *YOU!!*

To finish this chapter, I invite you to watch my message about the haters in your life. Most likely, they are people who love, or care about you, but they can't support you in the way you need them to, because they aren't you! It's time to silence the outside voices and tap into your own intuition. Learning how to make important decisions after paying attention to your inner voice and intuition is an important step on your path to #adulting and #youdoingyou, exactly how YOU want to!

Watch my video here: http://bit.ly/silencethehaters

# PART III.
# ALIGNMENT

CHAPTER 7

# #YouDoYou

---

*"What you think you become. What you feel, you attract. What you imagine, you create."*
—Buddha

## MEET NURIA

one of the most soft and loving people I've ever met. She is careful and deliberate with her words, and every one is thought out before she says it. Nuria is the quintessential walking heart. She is a giver, a supporter. Nuria shines brightly, but in terms of alignment she woke up one day and didn't recognize her own life. Nuria had been living a life that simply put was not "her." This is something I believe many of you reading this book will relate to. When I first met Nuria, she was living an unfulfilled life. A college graduate, she had been working as a legal assistant for six years and was unclear about the direction of her life.

Nuria knew her vision for her life financially was not aligned with her behaviors. By the time she'd scheduled her first call with me, she had accumulated about $12,000 in credit card debt and it was freaking her out. She felt like she was drowning. She had never had so much debt, and it did not match her vision of being financially stable. It was causing her a lot of pain. She knew better than to be in debt, but there she was with a pile of bills she couldn't figure out how to repay. Like Maya Angelou said, (a favorite quote of mine) "When you know better. You do better." She thought she knew how to do better, but she wasn't doing better and it was draining her emotionally.

She was going out too much, overeating, and using retail as therapy. She would spend beyond her means, buying shoes and clothes, and give her money away to other people. She was in a cycle using the majority of each paycheck to pay off credit card debt, then turning around and charging everything to her credit card because she didn't have any cash. She thought she was slowly getting ahead because she would pay off big chunks of debt at a time, but what she didn't realize was that she was sinking further and further. She was spending over $500 on her dog every month because she'd adopted a special needs animal. That's just who she is.

The stress of her overspending and lack of clarity on the direction of her life wasn't empowering or inspiring in her relationships either. Her debt had her feeling ashamed and embarrassed and she wasn't speaking up for herself. Saying "yes" to going out to happy hours, concerts, and weekend trips when her bank account and debt said "no," and staying silent to her partner about how she was struggling to make ends meet, she lived in a state of fear around money. All because she didn't yet understand how to make money work for her.

Can you relate? Maybe you're ashamed of your debt? Maybe you know you have a spending problem and find yourself hiding your new shoes, or handbag. Do you sneak them into the house when your loved ones aren't home, or hide them in the car? I've been there too! You're not alone and neither was Nuria.

But she *felt* alone.

She wasn't using her voice. She wasn't calling herself forward. In her eyes, she knew she wasn't being financially responsible and avoiding the problem was making it worse for her emotionally. By the time Nuria and I had our first meeting in person she felt broken, scared, ashamed, and embarrassed. She was exhausted and overwhelmed and (so) ready for a change. Like many of my clients she didn't know where to start. Showing up was the start, and here's what has happened as a result.

Because of our first meeting, Nuria realized she was holding herself small in her relationships and financially. That's what was causing her so much pain. She had stopped living her life perfectly aligned with her own vision and she felt lost and confused. SHE STOPPED LIVING FOR HERSELF and was LOST in a tangled web of supporting others. The first objective we discussed after I let her have a good cry was how to get clear about what she really wanted out of life. When you are aligned with your goals, it is infinitely easier to stay focused to make them happen.

After going through the same exercise (What's Important About Money To You) that I use with all my clients, it became painfully clear that Nuria wants to be a mom. She's in her early 30s and although her career is important, it's not as important as her want and desire to have a family. She's been lost in the hustle and shuffle of work and supporting her partner, and she had neglected the very thing she wanted most. After our conversation, she had to think long and hard about the other aspects of her life that were going to support her want and desire to have children.

It wasn't easy. It took many coaching sessions for her to connect her desire to be successful in a career and be financially independent with her desire to be a mother. Seven months later, she's a lot closer to her goal than she was the first time we met. She also realized that no matter her marital situation or her situation with or without children, she would always want to be out of debt. She would always want to be happy with her career choice. Although she could not control her current relationship status or whether or not she was pregnant, she could focus on the aspects of her life she could control <u>even if doing so only temporarily allowed her to feel better about her financial situation, and that's just what she did</u>, knowing each step was significant to her bigger vision. Similar to the story of the tortoise and the hare, slow and steady wins the race. Every small shift and change has brought her closer to her goals of financial freedom.

She stopped spending money on shoes. She started meal planning at home, and stopped eating out. She stopped binge eating and overindulging (in general). And she stopped charging on her credit card temporarily. When she stopped aimlessly shopping, she honored and celebrated her new decision! Nuria learned it's not only important to recognize your own financial power, but when you stick to your goals, you SHOULD celebrate! Getting closer to such an immensely important aim was definitely worth making a toast to herself!

Most importantly, Nuria took responsibility in her personal relationships. She started having new and responsible conversations with her significant other about money and future goals. She also set new boundaries with friends who overindulged and overspent. She didn't do it alone. She had a lot of coaching in the process, and changes didn't happen overnight.

Nuria is committed to paying down her debt. She set a goal to pay off $5,000 in credit card debt in three months and she's using all her spare time to work part-time jobs to pay it down fast. She is willing to do whatever it takes, and is accepting of the fact that debt is sometimes necessary in life even though it scares her.

# She's got a great plan she is sticking to consistently.

Keeping her promise to herself is in alignment with her being responsible. She's also working toward purchasing her first home that will help her build her net worth. I teach the women in my mentorship the importance of investing in themselves and Nuria decided she wants to diversify the ways she's investing in herself to achieve her new goal of building wealth.

It's important to mention here, that as Nuria made changes, her vision changed, too. She set bigger goals. Visioneering is an ongoing process. Just like standing in the gap is an ongoing commitment. Don't get stuck thinking you "reach someplace" and then stop growing. It's an evolving journey.

The beauty of visioneering is when you create a vision out of who you're being, and what you do, you can have change every day. But your core being doesn't necessarily have to change. Because it's not attached to what you have. You're not chasing a $10-million home. You're just waking up being who you want to be. It's totally okay to renegotiate with yourself in the interest of continuing to serve your changing desires for your life and profession.

The other thing I want to note here, is debt isn't always bad. When it is out of balance and not aligned it's bad. For example, Nuria committed to coaching, because it was an investment in herself and her worth. It was a way for her to align to who she authentically is and what she wants in her life. She is clearer than she's ever been about her intent to make her money work for her and not against her.

Let's talk about the three types of investments. As we dive in, you will learn exploring where you are and what you have put into these investments is a great way to figure out where you are in alignment and where you are not. The three types of investments are:

- Money.
- Time.
- People.

When Nuria was looking for part-time work, she had an opportunity to get paid $15 an hour. I said, "Is that worth your time?" Initially, she replied, "No, I don't believe it will be." But after we ran the numbers, she realized the job (even though she believes she's worth much more than $15 an hour), is a great way for her to use the money (she would be making) to pay down her debt. It was a decision she was willing to make because she was willing to do whatever it took to get out of debt. She is working odds and ends jobs consistently, and the value of that (also) is she's not spending time ineffectively. She is not out spending money because she is out earning it. That also plays a large role into how quickly she will meet her financial goals.

Nuria has had to make difficult decisions about her financial situation, work, and relationships. She's not the only client I have who has made significant changes in her life due to gaining clarity over the direction of her life and finances. She realized she couldn't afford to be around people who didn't fully support her and her desires. She has learned to speak up for herself and remove the people from her life who are not supportive of her dreams. Although her worth is not defined by how much debt she does or doesn't have, her worth is directly related to her relationship with herself and her relationship to money.

## You must wisely invest your time with people who are going to support you, lift you up, and help you create what you want to create.

If you are committed to being compassionate, but you're not surrounded by compassionate people, you need to find a new tribe. If you find yourself stressing out at that prospect, don't worry because I discuss your tribe in Chapter 12.

Again, it comes back to committing to who you're being. If you commit to being healthy, you are going to invest your time and money into being healthy. You will see a return on that investment although it may be frightening, like hiring a personal trainer is sometimes scary. You're going to renegotiate your time similar to the way you'd spend your time at a gym versus a bar.

I can't repeat this enough:

## Money is not about your success with money.

It's about how successful you feel about your life. And that comes down to how aligned you decide you want to be and who will be in alignment with you. True wealth and success isn't just about having more stuff or having more money.

You can have a lot of money and still be a doormat.

# **EXERCISE**

## #YouDoYou

Do the following exercise:

Based on your previous chapter's answers to who you are being, create two columns:

1. What behaviors support your being?

2. What behaviors do not support your being?

| (INSERT WHO YOU ARE BEING) ||
|---|---|
| Behaviors Supporting My Desired Being | Behaviors That Do Not Support My Desired Being |
|  |  |
|  |  |
|  |  |
|  |  |
|  |  |
|  |  |
|  |  |
|  |  |

3. Then take a stock-take of your behaviors that are *aligned* and those that are *misaligned* and do the following:

   - Commit to *stopping* behaviors that are misaligned.

   - Commit to *adopting* behaviors that are aligned.

CHAPTER 8

# Reckless Vs. Responsible

*"At the center of your being you have the answer: you know who you are and what you want."*
—Rumi

PEOPLE WHO ARE RESPONSIBLE for owning their "$hit" with clear focus, take committed action regardless of how they feel because the decisions they make arise out of their vision for their lives. That's why #visioneering is so important. It is imperative that to have your financial life working, you must understand why you do the things you do, why they matter, and which direction they are taking you in your life. Responsible people are responsible when it comes to what is important to them, no matter the cost. Sometimes, easy money is not the right money. Sometimes, the easy way, like showing up to work every day at a job you hate just because it's safe and secure isn't the responsible thing to do. You are not being honest with yourself if you hate your job! Although most people would say it is the responsible action to take because it pays the bills. I say that for you to really love your life you have to be willing to risk financial responsibility temporarily to make new commitments to yourself.

That is scary, but that's responsible to your truth, your hopes, and your dreams.

In comparison, reckless behavior is not grounded in purpose. It is the "fuck it" attitude people have about their lives, health, and finances. When someone is being reckless with their money and/or life, they are not grounded in a vision for themselves, and they often sabotage their success. It doesn't mean they are breaking laws or being deviant. What it means is that compared to who they really are or what they really want in life they aren't making decisions to support those aspirations. They spend money on stupid shit and make decisions that lead them down paths that aren't the best for them. Reckless is the equivalent of the shiny red ball syndrome. People who are reckless lack focus and clarity. They make decisions out of their past (looking back) and usually out of fear, sometimes even out of feelings rather than intentional focus. Reckless is often the "easy way out," but it comes with long-lasting consequences that may not result in what a sister really wants.

We are all susceptible to this. Reckless doesn't mean driving drunk in this context. A reckless action or decision is one that moves you away (not toward) your financial goals and ideal life. In a previous chapter, I talked about how you can get back on track by getting comfortable with being uncomfortable. It's okay to be afraid of change. Fear is an indicator of growth. In this chapter, I talk about having daily reset buttons in your life, so you can identify for yourself what is responsible behavior and what is reckless. With this new information, you can take steps toward living the life you say you really want. From reckless to responsible requires you to rewire your whole life. This takes time, effort, work, dealing with the haters, and it will not happen overnight. But I promise you that by taking steps toward your goals and vision you will get there, and your life will be more amazing than you can possibly imagine.

The first thing to uphold, is not to fall into too much self-judgment when you find out you have been reckless. For example, "I'm super pissed I have debt." You can be pissed. You can beat yourself up. You can have unworthy conversations, just like the best of them. You might tell yourself, "I'm not worthy. I'm ashamed. I know better."

But those are self-defeating, limiting conversations that when we have them keep us in reckless behaviors. The further down that rabbit hole we go, the easier it is to avoid our challenges, and say, "I'm never going to get out of debt. It's too hard." To get out of this trap, you must realize the following:

## You are <u>not</u> your debt.
## You are not your mistakes.

That one little reminder whether it's debt, whether it's a living situation or a relationship, is to remind yourself that you are not "this." "This" is an undesired outcome of your reckless behavior because you've not been responsible to the greatness that you are, to the light that you are.

It's often easier to charge a purchase on a credit card than to look at these facts about ourselves, than to look at the dynamics that aren't working, specifically. Remind yourself when you make a new commitment to be responsible you're going to have wreckage to clean up. But that wreckage doesn't define you. *That wreckage isn't YOU.*

That's why we need daily reminders. Just because you set your intentions that day, it doesn't mean you're done, you're good. There must be daily reminders and daily reset buttons because what you're doing, ultimately, moving from reckless to responsible, is rewiring your life. We need check-ins and resets. That's why I believe in the value of coaching because whenever I get off track I go right back to my coach; we talk about what's going on, reassess, and refocus.

The daily reset buttons are those daily meditations. Listening to Abraham Hicks is one of my favorite ways to reset. A 10-minute Abraham Hicks' talk will reset me. You can also take a nature walk. The most brilliant minds do this; it's not just my idea. When Einstein was tapped out on creativity, he rode his bike.

Tony Robbins talks about stepping away from chaos. The greatest minds will say you have to turn your brain off and you must get present and let your brain do work subconsciously. That's another reset. I call it matching behavior. In the moment, it's stopping. Let's say you're in the middle of Target, asking yourself, "How does this match my commitment?" That's an example you can use. It's very conscious behavior. If you're at Target and you grab something you want, think about your vision and ask yourself: Does this purchase move me closer to my vision or away from my vision?

You're constantly matching the world experiences and choices that make sense to your vision. That's the responsibility I'm talking about. You're being responsible for yourself, and those resets are a great way to live responsibly so you can have everything you want in your life.

# EXERCISE

## Reckless Vs. Responsible

In a previous chapter, we listed the behaviors that support who you want to be in the world, and the behaviors that don't support them.

The most important behaviors to address and shift quickly, are the ones that are reckless, and that have the most negative impact on your vision. It all depends on your vision. For example, some behaviors might be: not paying bills on time, continually charging on your credit card, or buying and eating more food when you feel down emotionally. For others, it could be *not* investing in that massage or self-care you deserve, hoarding too much money, and not investing in your well-being, or *not* saying no to a toxic relationship.

## Being compassionate includes having compassion for yourself.

Go back to that list, and put a *red flag* on reckless behaviors. Then, write down the *responsible* behavior instead. That means when you are in the world, you are matching and looking for opportunities to shift your behaviors.

# CHAPTER 9
# The Easy Way

*"All that glitters is NOT gold."*
—Unknown

BEFORE I TALK ABOUT THE "EASY WAY," I'm going to talk about the hard way. Because there are so many pitfalls to the hard way. First and foremost, there is the thinking you can do it on your own even though you have no experience. So, financially, the "hard way" is, that people will spend 10 years trying to figure out how to fix their money situation on their own.

They'll read a book; they'll talk to non-experts; they'll take advice from people who really don't understand their situation. They'll just think that, for whatever reason, they can do it on their own because it's how they've done everything their whole life. Weight loss is a great example of this. People think they can do it on their own. "I'm just going to go to the gym," they say, "I'm just going to show up." But they really don't know anything about fitness or nutrition.

I'm guilty of that. I've been an athlete my whole life and I'm blessed to have a petite figure. I don't know anything about nutrition. Despite that, I think I am pretty healthy. I walk my dog in the mornings. I've been a vegetarian for 20 years, but no matter what I do on my own, I still can't seem to get my pre-baby abs back! Instead of hoping that my investment of time "working out" will give me the results I want, I decided to take the easy way and hire an expert who can guarantee me the results I want because she knows how to get me there. It's a perfect exchange of my money for time.

So, the "hard way" would be for me to keep doing what I'm doing. Maybe I'll get some results, but it's a total guessing game. The same concept applies to our finances. When we're in debt, we're not making enough or we're in a living situation that's not working for us and the "hard way" is to think that somehow, by reading a book, that our whole life is going to be fixed.

My personal experience is that people believe by watching *Oprah*, *Ellen* or other thought leaders, we're going to get what we need to transform our lives. The problem is that when we take these actions we think we're improving ourselves but really, the information and content is not specific enough to our own lives to make a real difference.

You're implementing cookie-cutter solutions when you subscribe to that belief. At some point, you're going to come up against it and get stuck because your life is unique. It is like no one else's and so the way that you are with your money is going to be different from anybody else you know because you have different paths. You have different conversations that spark epiphanies. You have different debts. You have different people in your life. It's all unique. That's one of the biggest lies in the financial industry, IMO.

Take one of the wealthiest men in the world, Warren Buffett, for example. You can't do exactly what he did because you're not him.

You can't follow his footsteps to the letter. His success will never be your success because you're not him. You haven't lived his life.

You didn't invest when he invested. You're not as old as Warren. It's impossible for you to try to replicate his life and successes.

You have your unique talents and he has his. When it comes to money, trying to follow someone and assuming that if you do exactly what they do you'll get the same results is the hard way. It doesn't work like that.

You've seen people take weight loss advice from someone who's medically obese. When that happens, I react like: "I don't think that's going to work." It's not a personal attack, but it seems like reaching out to your immediate circle rather than someone who is an expert and has demonstrated personal results would be a detrimental and ineffective way to go.

For example, I love my family but they're not like me. Because they're nothing like me, taking advice from them feels like I'm hitting my head against the wall. Not because I don't love them but because they don't think like me.

The people who love us the most want to help us. We want to get help from people who love us but at the end of the day it's convoluted. Their love for us doesn't mean they can help us. That's a hard pill to swallow.

## Just because they love us, doesn't mean they can help us.

How can a person make changes to do things the easy way? First, admit you don't know how to go about your plan and that you need help. Number two, find help from people who have gotten where you want to go and who can teach you how to do it for yourself.

For example, Danielle, who I mentioned before, had never invested in herself prior to being my client. She was scared. Really,

really scared. As in, "Oh my gosh, I can't believe I'm going to do this." She told me, "I've never hired a coach before." People in her life doubted her for doing it. They said, "Don't do it, it's too much money." That was the kind of reception her circle gave her.

I could tell Danielle was checking me out at our first meeting and that she was a bit petrified. She is a totally different woman today than she was back then. When we first sat down and I asked Danielle questions in our initial session, it took her an exceptional amount of time (5-10 seconds) to answer. When she did, she kept her arms crossed and didn't lean in to fully participate in the conversation. She overanalyzed her responses. Now, Danielle opens up and shares how she is doing and what she needs each time we talk.

Despite her fears at letting me in, she pushed herself to work with me because she had come to me as a referral and was familiar with me; she knew I got clients results. She knew, somehow, I was going to help her get to the next level financially. She was in debt and realized she wasn't the expert. She didn't know how to get herself the results she wanted because if she did she would have had them already. Instead, she got real and asked herself, *if I don't do anything, if I keep going down the hard road, doing things as I've always done them, where's my life going to be?*

Here's another example. As you are reading this book right now, and as I'm writing it, I'm working with a writer. I knew to get this message out to you faster I had to hire somebody who knew how to get me there quicker and I was willing to pay him for it. It would have taken me three years to complete this book, but instead, I hired a writer. You're reading this book today because of him.

Seek people who know how to get you the results you want. Find someone who knows your problems, and who understands your problems. Someone who is not a cookie-cutter and who knows how to work with you as an individual and not give a one-size-fits-all approach. There is no such magic bullet. But in the self-help industry there's a lot of that mentality. The whole, "If you just do it my way, it'll work out." Ultimately, the communication is, "If you can be more like me then you can be more like you." Which is bullshit.

It's not to say stories aren't useful. They're great and inspiring. But you can't go back and try to replicate what's in those stories exactly because your life is nothing like the people who have lived them. You have to find people who can modify those stories to fit your life.

# EXERCISE

## Get Help

Invest in help. It's less risky this way. When you take a risk with a coach, or take the risk to get help, that risk is a lot lower than not doing anything. It's a higher risk to continue doing what you've been doing especially if what you've been doing isn't working.

When you are looking for a coach, make sure the person has credibility. They must know what they are talking about. Check their credentials.

You also want someone who takes the time to dig deep to understand what's important to you and who will help you gain clarity over where you're headed in life. Define what it is that you want. A lot of people find when they are talking about their life and business, it's a hard question to answer.

The second step is getting help in planning out a roadmap. You need this map, because if you can see the big picture, your questions become, "But what do I have to do next? What do I have to do in two hours?" Your coach must help you chunk those steps down into a roadmap. Then, when you are out there taking action, they can help you course correct and stay on track.

I ask my clients, "Is this is what you want?" And they say, "Yes, this is what I want." I then reply, "I'm only going to hold you there, where you will be accountable to what you say you really want. When I see you making choices that take you off your path, I'm going to ask your permission to interrupt you and help you course correct when needed, I'm the person in your life who is going to help you make choices in the direction of your dreams, no matter how hard it is, no matter how much you want to quit. That is my job. You are paying me to repeat to you what you want, and as you're navigating through the experiences and the relationships and the people and the decisions, the only thing that I'm doing is matching to what you want. My job is helping you figure it out along the way. *And, to never give up on you. Even when you feel like giving up on yourself.*"

# PART IV.
# ACTION &
# ACCOUNTABILITY

CHAPTER 10

# Be Savage

---

*"When I loved myself enough, I began leaving whatever wasn't healthy. This meant people, jobs, my own beliefs and habits—anything that kept me small. My judgment called it disloyal. Now I see it as self-loving."*
—Unknown

I WANT TO SHARE WHAT BEING A SAVAGE IS NOT. Women have very different relationships with power and money than men. Women are often not forceful or direct because of the many ways that we have been called out in our lives for being either pushy or bossy. How many times has a strong woman unnecessarily been called a bitch?

We have a very hard time being socially forward because of the way it's perceived. So many of us avoid assertiveness because it can be perceived incorrectly. Those perceptions are hurtful. They create a negative impact because that's not who we are. We don't want to be seen that way.

Being savage, does not mean that you are a horrible human being or that you are ruthless or doing whatever it takes to get ahead, like walking over people. It is not that. It's not being a sociopath. It's not giving the middle finger and telling everybody "I'm just going to do my own thing." That's not it.

When people wake up with the attitude, "Zero fucks given," that's an immature form of trying to be an individual.

There are many women who I look up to daily who perfectly embody what #savage means in the context of transforming your life. Take Jane Goodall for example. She is on a mission to conserve the environment, to save chimpanzees. She must wake up every single day caring more than anyone else cares about her causes. She doesn't wake up and say, "I give zero fucks." She wakes up every single day and asks herself, *what can I do to make a difference*? Being #savage means that she has to face incredible challenges and obstacles; she has to make people feel comfortable and fight daily to make a difference on this planet. But she cares a lot about humanity, and I know you do, too. Being #savage means caring enough about your life to stop and course correct, to do what it takes to have what you want so that you can also make a difference in your own life and on this planet.

## Being savage is being "Willing to give a f*ck."

There are ways of being that do not mean you will be a doormat. Savage people realize you can work with people while not being a pushover. Like standing in the gap, being savage is about developing the willingness to be uncomfortable. It means you are eager to do the hard work so you can become more responsible and be proud of yourself.

You must be willing to wake up and care more about what you want temporarily to get what you want long-term, and you have to be committed to shutting out the external voices. It doesn't mean you don't listen. It just means you don't let other people's opinions rule your life.

This applies even if a project or client is going to pay you a lot of money and it's not in alignment with who you are, that you are courageous and willing to make the decision to say, "No," to what's not aligning with you.

Being savage is waking up and saying, "I really don't love what my company does to the environment. It's more important to me that the environment is clean and that we have clean water than it is that my company's polluting it." Being savage is taking a stand to make a change in your life because it doesn't align with what you value.

I'll give you an example. I think the biggest risk I ever took financially was to leave my job at UNLV. My life was good. I made a decent salary, had great benefits, and I really loved the students. There wasn't anything "wrong." I could have stayed in that job for the rest of my life, and many people choose to do that. I would have been okay. I didn't hate it, but I knew there was a bigger calling for me. I could have a bigger impact on the planet. My decision came down to the fact I knew I wanted to work in different areas and that I wanted something bigger for my life.

So, I had to be savage enough and connected enough to myself to own up to the fact that even though there was nothing wrong, there wasn't a whole lot that was right, either, for what I wanted in my vision.

The second example is that I decided to go into the world of finance because I knew there would be financial opportunity. That's honest. People don't typically go into finance without thinking of the money.

So, I stayed in a high net worth firm working around millionaires because I knew eventually it was going to pay off. I was just doing it the hard way. I knew if I did it their way I would be rewarded, but it wasn't me. So, I had to be savage enough to say, "This isn't me anymore." It was nothing personal against anyone. It was about me taking a risk and being savage about what I wanted. I said, "I don't really know if this is going to work out but it's what I want and I'm going for it." I had to be willing to take a risk so I could live the life I wanted, the life I live today.

This is a prime example in my life of when I was scared. I was terrified, having no idea how my ex-husband was going to react. My thoughts were torture: *Am I crazy? How do I know this is what I really want? I'm not happy... I know I'm not happy... Isn't there another way?*

The important takeaway is understanding the type of risk you are going to accept. Not all risk is created equally. What I mean is that people will wake up one day and say, "F it, I'm going to move. It's what I want." But they won't put the right plans in place or give those plans the time they need to be successful. That's an irresponsible risk. Being savage is not taking a risk for the sake of risk-taking.

It's not for the exhilaration of the risk. It's that you see, in the world of investing, that there's an upside. Yes, there is always the potential it's not going to work out. That's life. But, when you follow what's true for you and when you do what you really love and really want, even a short-term failure is not a failure.

## A setback is not forever.

You have to quantify the risk. I'll bring it back to money. Investing in the stock market is a risk. A lot of people do it the hard way. They know nothing about the stock market, but they'll open up an

E-Trade account. They'll put a few thousand dollars in and start investing in stocks.

That's one way to take a risk and learn the hard way or you can find somebody to coach and mentor you in how to do it, because they've had success. You can hire them to teach you how to protect the downside of the risk so you don't lose it all overnight. But you have to be smart about it.

I've done things the hard way before. It really hurt. I survived it but that's how we learn. That's how we stay bigger than any challenge we have to face in life.

For example, I'm going through a divorce right now. It's a challenge I've had even while writing this book. But I didn't stop writing because of it. I know my book is part of playing a bigger game.

I realized that my marriage is not serving me at the highest levels. But I was at odds with myself because I had made a commitment 15 years ago when I met my ex and again, 12 years ago when we got married. The hard way has been pushing through because of a commitment, but ultimately, neither of us are happy.

Nothing was wrong. There was no abuse, no violence. But the stakes were high just the same. I have a nine-year-old. And so, do I stay in an unfulfilling marriage or do I go? I believe the hard way would be for me to stay in my marriage even though society says it's the right thing to do. Even though society's going to judge me, even though my son's going to go through some difficult times.

It took me being savage enough to have the conversation with my child. He's just as relieved as I am that I found the courage to speak up, because otherwise we might still be living unhappily together.

And we like each other, my husband and I; we actually really like each other. We just don't want to be married to each other anymore.

People will see our divorce however they want. I have to be willing to be vulnerable and judged. There are going to be haters out there.

## What's better for you and your vision is better for everyone.

As you are reading this right now, are you in a job or situation you hate, but you have chosen to stay? Are you living in a body you hate and you're not happy with it but you're not willing to do the hard work to get healthy? Are you avoiding bankruptcy because you're scared of the haters? *Everybody has skeletons in the closet.*

Personally, I thrive on being challenged. That's not everybody. I get that. That's exactly what I don't want, for you to read this book and go, "I have to do it the way Lisa does it," because not everybody is like me.

Embracing challenge has happened over time. It's not something that took place overnight. I started at a young age, testing, doing things my own way. I didn't always have desired consequences. We can use this framing as it pertains to the conversation about dealing with the haters or with my dad, in fourth grade. I wanted to go to a conference and he told me "No." I shot back, "Well, I'm going to go anyway."

Not everybody's like that. But, the power of being challenged means you're growing and that's why I believe in personal growth. When you challenge yourself, you have an opportunity to grow and that means you can move your life forward… and *that* means you can fulfill your destiny. But you can't do it if you don't challenge yourself.

That's why we go to school. We could all stay five-year-olds and never read a book, never move ourselves forward. But the woman who wants to give back in this world, must be willing to challenge herself so she can have new skills. She can have new talents and she can actually make a difference. She can't do that if she doesn't challenge herself. It all depends on who you want to *be*. That's the top of your vision.

That commitment can lead to magical results.

I'll give you an example. Kristi in her 40s, not exactly the Millennial woman but she's a Millennial woman because of the way she lives her life. She's an independent, hard-working gal, who came out of a divorce and struggled to be financially stable. I mean, she struggled hard. When she met me, she was not sure if she and her family were going to be able to keep their house or if she could support herself and her two kids.

She was a realtor who'd had a few great months, which caused her to call me. Since the Las Vegas real estate market took off earlier this year, she's has money for the first time in a very long time. When we talked, she said, " I need help now because I don't want to do anything to sabotage my life."

She took a risk by calling me, being vulnerable and saying, "I have money now and I don't know what to do with it. But I'm committed to my life being different, to moving forward. That means being financially stable forever, not just for now."

So, in the short amount of time she's worked with me she's gotten over $15,000 saved. She's literally been working with me for not even three months. She's paying all her bills, taking vacations, managing her money well, and her business is booming. Oh, and she attracted the love of her life.

In my playbook, I'm going to teach you a few simple and easy tactics you can apply to better manage your money. You can do them right now, and get started on your new financial path. The best course of action you can take today is to follow the path of understanding your value and purpose on this planet. Then back up your beliefs with sound and stable money management practices. I share the ones that make the biggest differences in my clients' lives in chapter 11—The Playbook.

Your life doesn't have to be a train wreck to hire a coach.

## Being savage is being willing to say, "I want more."

I want more. I want more love. I want more joy. I want to give more. I want to have more money. You have to be willing to do that. It's super savage and sexy as hell, when a woman says, "I want more."

Ask yourself:

1. What do you want more of?
2. What is the gap between where you are today and where "more" actually is? The better your gap is defined, the easier it will be to set and achieve goals.
3. If you got "more," how would you feel?
4. What's stopping you from having more today?

It is okay to want more. You deserve more! It's time for you to have more, and if you don't hear this from anyone else in your life, I want you to hear it from me that *more is good*. More is not self-indulgent. More means more love, more money, more kindness, more experiences. These are all things that everyone wants and the sooner you can stop denying yourself what you really want in life, the sooner you can get to living the life you were meant to live!

CHAPTER 11

# Playbook

---

*Life is a song - sing it. Life is a game - play it. Life is a challenge - meet it. Life is a dream - realize it. Life is a sacrifice - offer it. Life is love - enjoy it.*
—Sai Baba

YOU MIGHT HAVE THOUGHT MY ENTIRE BOOK was going to be a playbook filled with financial guidance and tips for young women. But here's the truth. Unless you know who you are, and where you're headed in life, it is incredibly difficult to make choices with your money.

If money is the car you are going to drive through life, how will you make decisions about the kind of car you're doing to drive? The first action you must take is to get clear about the lifestyle you live and where you'll be driving the car before you can make a conscious decision about the right car for you.

It's the same way with money. You can't make clear and conscious decisions about what to do with your money until you have CLARITY over the direction of your life!

My hope is by the time you're reached this point in the book, you've done the exercises in the previous chapters. You've done some work to explore the purpose and direction of your life and who will be in your life to support you along the way. By now you're ready to make the connection to your money, so that when you sit down to make sense of your finances you'll have a solid understanding of why these decisions matter in the first place.

Maybe you've discovered you're worth more than what you're getting paid and it's FINALLY time to pursue the career you've always wanted. Maybe you've realized you're stuck in that relationship or have not taken the risk to travel to your number one destination, that you, like me, have been telling yourself you don't have enough money to see, but you actually DO! Like Valerie, another one of my clients, it has been your limiting belief about money that has stopped you from having the life you really want—NOT THE MONEY itself.

I'm here to tell you that no matter the financial situation you're in and no matter the life situation you're facing, if you are truly ready to make the changes you desperately want in your life and with your money that it is 100 percent POSSIBLE. When you follow these simple and easy-to-use plays in my playbook you'll begin to create clear and confident financial clarity and progress toward your goals. This is the playbook I use with all my clients and I promise that as soon as you make the connection to your purpose and direction in life, you WILL begin to make new and empowering choices with your money.

Ready to take charge, and get confident with your money?

Don't wait, follow this playbook and let's get started!

## Separate Your Money

If you're anything like my clients, you likely bank out of one account. It's the same account that you're simultaneously paying bills out of AND spending out of. There is lack of clarity about what your transactions are, what money is going out, what money is coming in, and it's very difficult to understand what you're spending each month because it's all jumbled together.

If you do nothing else after reading this book, this ONE thing will save you money, time, and a headache when trying to make important financial decisions.

You need to separate the money that you pay your bills with, from the money that you spend with. My clients have many creative ways they do this. You can start with using the KISS Your Money Sheet that you can grab as a part of my book bonuses! Grab the sheet here: www.ADULTINGYOURWAY.com

Take the time to fill out the sheet so you have a clearer understanding of what your fixed bills versus your flexible money is each month. When you separate your money, you get clearer about what money you MUST have each month to pay bills, and then you can begin to make decisions about the money you have that's left each month.

Separating your money into different accounts based on how you spend your money (i.e., fixed bills versus grocery money) will help you stay focused and you will have a better understanding of the activity in each account. My clients tell me this is a life saver!

## Tackling Debt

You can have a life AND pay off debt!!

What's most important for you to understand about debt is that you didn't get into debt overnight, and you will not get out of debt overnight. To successfully pay off debt you must do three things:

## 1. BE WILLING TO LIVE WITHIN YOUR MEANS AND REORGANIZE YOUR LIFE WHEN AND WHERE NEEDED SO YOU CAN DO SO.

Remember Danielle? She decided to live with her parents so she could pay off debt and save for her home. Another client was willing to move into an apartment because she could save a few hundred dollars per month to pay down debt and save at an even faster rate.

## 2. HAVE A CLEAR AND ATTAINABLE STRATEGY IN PLACE.

Debt will only get paid off and stay paid off if you have a clear and attainable strategy in place. If you're anything like me, you get daily offers in the mail to consolidate your debt. Be wary of offers that seem too good to be true. Many of the offers will lock you into a monthly payment that is not negotiable and there are fees tacked on to the backend of the debt restructuring. Although it may seem like a great way to consolidate your debt, it may not be the best solution. Look at all your options and be sure to consult an expert before you make any decisions. Not all debt is created equally, and you need to do a thorough analysis of the best ways to pay off your debt most efficiently. It will take commitment, time, and restructuring your life to pay it off and keep it off forever. I don't recommend going at it alone. Get help. Most importantly, you must be willing to make temporary sacrifices (not forever sacrifices) to get out of debt. You must be willing to ask for help. You must be willing to follow this next step—or you will never be out of debt.

Getting out of debt requires crystal-clear commitment and strategy. Your goals must be attainable. If you're anything like some of my clients the first thing they want to do with any extra money that comes their way (e.g., tax return, inheritance, bonus) is to put 100 percent of it toward debt. It would be best for you to chunk out that money instead, so you can progress toward all your goals in life. For example, one of my client's husbands just received his year-end bonus. The first thing they wanted to do was throw all that money at their credit card debt. The problem with that is that they won't be able to enjoy any of the money he worked hard for. AND, they will still not have any money in emergency savings. This type of strategy: "Throw it all at debt," will only keep them in debt. After looking at their financial picture, they decided to pay off three credit cards totaling $1,100. They are going to give $1,000 to themselves for Christmas and date nights (even though they are in debt, they can still enjoy their lives!), and the rest they will place into an emergency reserve fund so they can stop using their credit cards for good.

We established a long-term debt repayment strategy that will get them out of debt in a few years and at the same time they will have a balanced and livable strategy that will help them to live healthy and vibrant lives. That is a win-win debt repayment strategy.

## 3. PUT THE CARDS AWAY FOR GOOD!

You will not be able to get out of debt using the same behaviors that got you into debt. Remember Danielle? She only got out of debt, and will continue to stay out by creating new spending and saving habits! She has stopped using her cards completely, but she had to break the cycle. If you are serious about getting out of debt, then you need to be serious about not consuming debt. This is not a forever strategy, but it will help you stop your current spending habits and behaviors so you can rewire your habits. Let's schedule a call if you're ready to talk about how to implement any of these strategies into your own life.

## STOP SPENDING YOUR MONEY ON STUPID $HIT

You have needs and wants in your life. The problem persists when you are unclear about what you need versus what you really want. When you lack clarity in your spending habits it is very likely that you are spending money on stupid shit (aka things that don't matter now, and probably never will!) Many people (and I know because I've done this myself) walk into Target and Walmart with an internal conversation going something like this:

YOU, walking into Target: "Okay, I'm only going in for toilet paper, hairspray, makeup remover, and shampoo. I'm going to avoid the dollar section!"

YOU, walking through Target: "Oh my gosh, that is so cute, and it's only a dollar! Okay, I'm going to get it. I'm going to use it. I don't really need it but I want it and it's only a dollar!"

YOU, walking out of Target: "How in the world did I just spend $100?"

Sound familiar!?!? The truth is that $100 adds up over time. If you do this every month, you are spending $1,200 on stupid shit! In reality, if you were more strategic with money you could be sitting on a beach in Cancun—and I know you would much rather do that!

Take some time to reflect on the things in your house you bought randomly, the clothing in your closet with the tags on it, the nights eating out, or the Starbucks coffees you've consumed. If you could go back and put all that money together could you have taken that trip you've always dreamed of, or finally gone back to school because you could have invested that money in your education to become the entrepreneur or author you've always dreamed of becoming?

The point of this play is for you to examine your spending behaviors and reengineer the way money flies out of your bank account. The best thing you can do for yourself right now is own up to all the things you spend money on that do not add value to your life. Once you do that, ask yourself, *what is really important to me, and how am I going to make it happen financially? How am I going to stop spending money on stupid shit*? I promise you, freedom is on the other side of this valuable and worthwhile conversation.

## TELL YOUR CASH FLOW YOU'RE THE BOSS!

You must get a handle on your cash flow. One of the reasons you might be feeling so disorganized with your financial life is that you don't have a good understanding of how money flows through your household monthly. This means that some weeks you have excess money and others you're overdrafting because you aren't keeping track of the bills you've paid and you're not effectively anticipating bills going out month-to-month.

This is a very common problem with my clients. They haven't learned how to manage their "books" and it is causing pain and pressure throughout the month. The technique I share with you below is going to differ for everyone because everyone gets paid at different times of the month so I will not go into detail about this specifically as it pertains to dates. My hope is that you'll get the idea of it, and start organizing your money. You know how to find me if you want help in the process.

The best way to understand your cash flow is to make a list (preferably in Excel) of all your bills and then organize them by due date. Next, insert when you'll be getting paid and how much you'll be getting paid by date. Do this for the next month. Your table will look something like this:

| 1 | PAYCHECK | $2,500.00 |
| 1 | HEALTH INSURANCE | $250.00 |
| 1 | POWER | $50.00 |
| 1 | CREDIT CARD 1 | $170.00 |
| 1 | WATER BILL | $35.00 |
| 1 | CREDIT CARD 2 | $70.00 |
| 2 | CELL PHONE | $70.00 |
| 5 | RENT | $1,100.00 |
| 5 | AUTO INSURANCE | $100.00 |
| 15 | PAYCHECK | $2,500.00 |
| 16 | INTERNET | $35.00 |
| 27 | CAR PAYMENT | $315.00 |

What do you notice from the above example? The majority of bills that are paid out each month are due at the front end of the month. Meaning, that one paycheck has an uneven distribution of bills for the month. If the person above is living paycheck-to-paycheck it makes complete sense that she feels broke between the 5th and the 15th of every month!

In order to successfully tell your cash flow who's the boss—YOU!—you must get a handle on how that money can be wisely spent and allocated between paychecks. The easiest way to do this is to list it out (as shown above), so you can understand what's leftover once all your bills are paid. Now, follow along with the chart below. Subtract the bills from the paycheck total and you'll know from each paycheck what you have to spend, invest or keep (save).

## GIRL, GET YOUR $HIT TOGETHER!

| 1 | PAYCHECK |  | $2,500.00 |
|---|---|---|---|
| 1 | HEALTH INSURANCE | $250.00 | $2,250.00 |
| 1 | POWER | $50.00 | $2,200.00 |
| 1 | CREDIT CARD 1 | $170.00 | $2,030.00 |
| 1 | WATER BILL | $35.00 | $1,995.00 |
| 1 | CREDIT CARD 2 | $70.00 | $1,925.00 |
| 2 | CELL PHONE | $70.00 | $1,885.00 |
| 5 | RENT | $1,100.00 | $755.00 |

| 5 | AUTO INSURANCE | $100.00 | $655.00 | <--------This is what you have to spend, invest or keep after this paycheck. |
|---|---|---|---|---|
|  |  |  |  |  |
|  |  |  |  |  |
| 15 | PAYCHECK |  | $ 2,500.00 |  |
| 16 | INTERNET | $35.00 | $ 2,465.00 |  |
| 27 | CAR PAYMENT | $315.00 | $ 2,150.00 | <--------This is what you have to spend, invest or keep after this paycheck. |

What a difference!!

This is the best exercise you can use to start understanding how to manage the money that you have coming in and out every month. After you've discovered "what's left" after each paycheck you can efficiently decide what to do with that money. All my clients have a spending plan and they separate their spending money from the money they have to spend on bills. Knowing "what's leftover" after each paycheck will successfully get you on track with your spending so you will feel more in control of your money month-to-month!

CHAPTER 12

# Find Your #Tribe

*"If you want to change the world, you have to be around people who are talking about changing the world and actually doing it."*
—Lisa Chastain

*WHAT IS YOUR TRIBE AND WHY SHOULD YOU FIND ONE?* Your tribe is those people in your life who are going to support you no matter what. For example, the content in *this chapter* was created because I leaned on *my tribe* of women (Allison, Brie, and Susana). We are women building businesses to empower other women, and we met at a mastermind where we all focused on *leveling* each other up. Especially in our businesses.

If you want to level-up in life, if you want to talk control, and you have a big dream, you must find people who are not just going to support you, but they must be people who will not drive you down.

Women coming together supporting women is special and somewhat unique. If you can find other women who are not going to have a pity party with you and not going to complain about their man, and not going to complain about what's wrong in their life, but who are all reaching for something, then they're going to keep each other focused, too.

Similarly, your tribe is a group of people who will hold you high and hold you accountable, and they won't pull you into distractions that will keep you from being who you want to *be* in the world. They will help you continue to move forward and propel you in life. This also includes challenging you.

Look at the five people closest to you and think about who they are, where they are, if they bring you up or hold you down? The five people closest to you who bring you up are your tribe. Those who don't *aren't* your tribe. It's simple as that.

I also want to add your tribe doesn't necessarily have to be on the *same level* or on a *bigger* level than where you are. How else could any tribe grow in number and strength? They must *want* to level up and be on a similar path as you. For example, find people who are passionate about what they are doing, whatever it is. That's the energy you want to be around.

The other thing about your tribe is you need a diverse group. People from all walks of life. Because that way you get to benefit from different perspectives, different expertise, etc. For example, Brie and I discussed that when you find the right tribe, you can hear *informal advice* from strong experts, you don't necessarily have to pay for. In exchange, you can provide *informal advice* they don't necessarily have to pay for.

How do you know when you have the right tribe? There's a saying: *Great minds discuss ideas; average minds discuss events; small minds discuss people.* The answer is: <u>when your conversation is about your goals and aspirations.</u>

Here's an excerpt of a conversation I had with members of my tribe.

> **Me:** The tribe are those people in your life who are going to support you no matter what, which is different in this context (women finding other women who are determined to grow and support each other together) because most people have a tribe.
>
> **Brie:** Some of my best friends at home are good for… you got a relationship issue… they can help you, but when it comes to business stuff…
>
> **Allison:** They totally can't.
>
> **Allison:** If they're not in the same place it's hard to even get advice from them if they don't get the whole picture.
>
> **Brie:** So, I think finding people… they don't necessarily have to be on the exact same level that you're at, but they have to want to be on the same level that you want to be at. I think that's more important. One of my girls right now, we just went to a Tony Robbins thing together, and she invested in this real estate class. She's selling right now and I'm so happy for her! She's probably financially where I was at a year ago, where she's just trying it out, and it's new and really exciting because we're gonna get to the same place. It's important to have people to talk to. Finding someone to support you when you're down is one thing, but finding somebody to support you when you're up, and they're not up… that's the tribe.
>
> **Me:** Finding other people who are passionate about what they're doing and pushing on based on passion.
>
> **Allison:** Yeah, I don't have many people who are like that really.

**Me:** People who are reckless, speed. People who are reckless, do drugs, that kind of stuff. My definition of reckless is someone who has a vision and has dreams but doesn't make choices for those things. That's reckless for them. But then they can't make empowered choices with their money because they're being reckless with their life and what they really want. So, being responsible is making choices with what you really want and finding the help that you need.

**Brie:** Like consciously upgrading your tribe?

**Me:** So, the tribe is not your homies, but people that you've always known. Your tribe are the fans, the sisters… Why is it important to find your tribe? Because if you want to level-up in life and you really want to talk control and you have a big dream, you have to find people who are not just going to support you but who are not gonna drive you down. How do you know you're in the right tribe? Well, if you are someone, which might help for this book, it is someone who's reading this book who wants to level up in life and they're ready to control their money, they're ready to live purposely. When you know you're around people who are talking about the same things that are important to you, right? I's not people who are talking about other people; it's not about people who are talking about things or drama or stuff or shit that's happened, but it's people who are talking about the next level and ideas and I always say that, if you want to change the world, you have to be around people who are talking about changing the world… whatever the world is.

**Allison:** So, your tribe is other people who want to move. You don't have to motivate them to move. You don't need to prove to them that they're worthy of something better.

They already know that and they're looking at how to get there.

**Me:** How do you know you've found the right tribe? Because you're around other women, I would say, because this book is written for women, other women who are doing big things with their life and that they can support you and love you and help you grow and understand your journey.

**Brie:** And be a cheerleader.

**Allison:** Call you on your shit.

**Me:** Here's another question. What happens if I find my tribe then eventually outgrow them?

**Allison:** I don't truly believe that you can fully outgrow your whole tribe. There has to be elements of your tribe, other members of your tribe that are still growing at the same rate that you are. It could be that your tribe just gets smaller within your tribe.

**Brie:** I think as you go and you grow you constantly need to be looking for people, like you just constantly need to be growing because I think that the more successful you get the smaller the options, so I think the more successful you get the more you have to keep your eyes open and make friends and network and change your relationships a little bit. You're still gonna have your friends, at whatever level they're at, it's not like you're gonna be like "Oh, excuse me, I moved from the 25 to 40K a month, tribe, so eff you."

**Me:** That's the fear, though. I have a lot of clients where when we talk about money beliefs that's one of their biggest fears that if I move up financially, I'm gonna have to leave these people behind.

**Allison:** Why can't it be that your tribe doesn't change but your role in the tribe does? Maybe initially your tribe was everybody keeping each other accountable, you're all helping each other, but maybe part of your role in the tribe is to nurture more of the people that aren't at that same level. So, they get up there. You're almost like, you give back a bit more, within your tribe to nurture your tribe.

**Me:** I think what it comes down to with the right tribe is accountability and holding people high. That's a leadership conversation, because as a leader we're going this way for women and that's what my whole book is about. My whole book is as women, we're gonna stand up and we're gonna propel the world forward, but we're all mutually pulling each other up. You don't necessarily outgrow your tribe but I think from a leadership perspective, as you grow you're bringing others up. You can't be afraid, and I talk about this in another chapter, you can't be afraid to let go of toxic people.

**Brie:** I don't have one shitty friend.

**Allison:** Yeah, I don't either.

**Brie:** I swear, when I decided that I would not have one shitty friend my life got better.

**Me:** That's the tribe. People often have misperceptions of what a coach is, let's tell them what it is not and does not do.

**Allison:** They're not gonna do the work for you.

**Me:** Totally, a coach is not gonna do it for you. That is not a coach, for sure.

**Allison:** That's hired help.

**Me:** That's an assistant. Hired help. They should work for you, be a W2 employee, and they're not someone that's gonna kiss your ass, either.

**Allison:** That's a horrible coach.

**Me:** Let's round it out. A coach is someone who holds you high, sees your potential, but coaches you where you're at, and also can coach you into making sure that you get the results you really want, and then the four of us are all testimonies to that. Your tribe with the right coach will keep you moving forward and that is the definition of transformation, that we're going somewhere, we're moving together, different ways, but then we have a coach that's gonna help us stay focused and keep moving.

When I first found my tribe at a mentorship, I listened to what all the women were creating and sharing. They were talking about taking control of their lives. Contributing. Playing a much bigger game. When I heard them talking and got swept up into their energy, *I knew I'd found my tribe.*

We're all growing. We all want something bigger but for us it's not just about ourselves. We don't want money for money's sake. A thrill does come from the money, but the real thrill comes from the impact you have on other people's lives. We are all jazzed.

Since you have read this book, I know you are someone who wants to level up in life and who wants to control your money. You want to live purposely by being who you want to be and aligning your behaviors with that intention. I know this journey has not been easy, it never is. But what I do know is that if you're willing to make an investment in time, money, and in yourself before anyone else, that you will begin to take steps (that at times will surprise you) to living the life you've been dreaming of. It is going to happen, don't give up on yourself. I won't give up in believing in you either.

Deal?

# CONCLUSION

MY HOPE IS THAT THROUGH THE PROCESS OF THIS BOOK you've done the work to take a look at your life, so you can answer the most important questions you need to answer to control your money, live purposefully, and love your life. By now you should be able to answer these questions:

Where are you today?

Where do you want to be?

Identify the gap between the two, get uncomfortable enough to face forward, face your fears, and go for what you really want!

I've spent 20 years coaching, advising and mentoring men and women who have each at one point in their lives said, "I really need to get my $hit together," and I've helped them each sort through the maze of their lives so they could silence the voices outside, listen to their true calling in life, and become successful by their own standards. THIS is what I want for YOU!

Today, after making a valuable investment in yourself by reading my book, taking time to ask the hard questions, and getting organized and clear about the direction of your life, your money should also make much more sense to you. Your money is your life; your life is your money. There is no way for you to separate what you want from how you spend, and let this serve as your wake-up call to make intentional and truth-seeking decisions for the rest of your life.

I wrote this book for you. The woman with insurmountable potential and light just waiting to burst wide open into the world to make a difference. You were born to leave a lasting legacy of love, hope, and inspiration, and today I am here to tell you that you CAN do it, and that with courage and the right people in your corner anything is possible in your life.

Gaining confidence and clarity with your money is just as important as taking care of your health. It affects your health! I know you're tired of staying up at night worrying about your money. I know how painful it is to be unclear and disorganized with your money. I know how hard it is to ask for help and I'm here to tell you that you're not alone. I, along with my SISTER tribe, promise you that it is 100 percent possible for you to have what you REALLY want in your life. Today is the day for you to make it happen.

This book is filled with nuggets and pearls of wisdom that I've learned myself over the course of my lifetime. You can always come back to it, and I can guarantee you that as your life continues to move in new directions, your need for clarity will evolve, too. What you've discovered about yourself in this book today is just one layer of many and I encourage you to revisit and keep working on yourself. It will pay off!

Finally, I invite you to join my world.

If you really do want results, if you really are ready to get to work, roll up your sleeves and make your life even more amazing than it is today, I am here to mentor you. I tell my clients (and it's true!) that I they are my full-time job. I designed my life exactly as I love it, and doing exactly what I believe I was put on this earth to do... help women just like you to control their money, live purposefully, and to LOVE their lives! My invitation stands. Please join my SISTER Mentorship and take that next step to being authentically, bravely and beautifully you.

Safe travels, choose the light, and know that I'm always here cheering you on.

—Lisa

# ACKNOWLEDGEMENTS

THERE ARE SO MANY PEOPLE who have supported me on this journey, and I'm grateful for each and EVERY one of you!

Thank you Connor, my son, my light, my motivation. You are my "why" and I'm so grateful that you've let me stay up late, wake up early, be cranky with you and loved me through this.

Mom and Dad, I am who I am because of you. I am grateful each and every day that you continue to love and support me... even though we may not always agree. I love you so much. Thank you for giving me the best life you knew how to give. I will forever be grateful.

To my best friends, Genevieve, Kristine, Tania, Susan, Greg, Ashley, Kodi, Ryun, Quinn, Jeffi, and countless others... I could not have done this without your love and support. Your texts, calls, voicemails, funny facebook posts and most importantly your unwavering love for me got me through the really tough days. I appreciate you and will forever love you!

To the Book Launch Team - holy moly! This thing is complete in record time because you took the time to give me honest feedback and you kicked my ass with honesty. Thank you for taking time to care, thank you for your thoughts, and thank you for being my biggest cheerleaders! Drinks on me next time I see you!

To my coaches - Robyn, Trevor, Ashley, Jon, and Hilary - WOW!! You're an incredible support system of experts and I COULD NOT have found a more loving and capable group of people to work with. Robyn, you especially have transformed my life with love and friendship. I thank God every day for you. Thank you for being my mentors and for believing in me, even when I did not believe in myself.

To the FEMMs... you're amazing! We are in this fight to make this world a more loving and healthy place. You inspire me to wake up and make it happen, I am grateful for your courage, wisdom and sisterhood!

Finally, to my SISTERS. You're the real hero's in this world. Mothers, sisters, daughters, leaders, friends and amazing human beings who are taking your lives on.

I am honored to be your coach, thank you for your trust in me and confidence that with my guidance you will get what you want. You already are and continue to do so. Never give up, I will never give up on YOU!

# GIRL, GET YOUR $HIT TOGETHER!

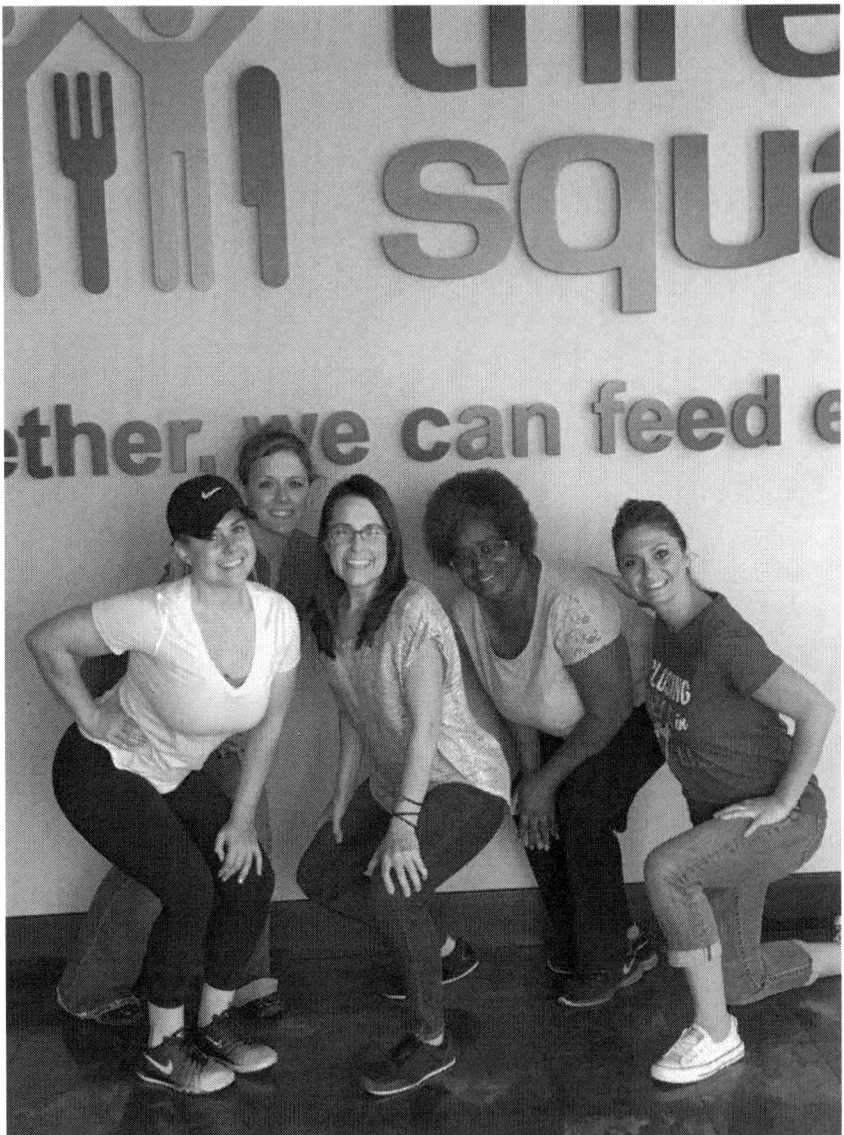
ether, we can feed

# PRODUCTS AND SERVICES

## SISTER MENTORSHIP:

Strong Independent Successful Talented Empowered RESULTS

For a Financially Secure Future

Inviting brilliant women who are ready to take on their lives.

Join me for 6 months - seats are limited. Let's talk ASAP.

## SCHEDULE A FREE 15 MINUTE DISCOVERY CALL TODAY

lisachastain.setmore.com

# ABOUT THE AUTHOR

LISA HAS DEDICATED HER LIFE to making a difference for people. Starting as young as she can remember, she's had a knack for breaking down complex systems into common language that anyone can understand. Lisa is a lifelong giver and learner, and through her journey as a peer, mentor, career and academic advisor, life coach, and financial advisor, she is now living her life on purpose and teaching others to do the same."

In late 2016, Lisa left her firm to start her own company as a Millennial Money Coach so she could help people transform their lives and relationships with money. She helps her clients learn exactly where their money goes each month and how they can get out of the rat race

Lisa is your go-to mentor. She will focus on your "big picture," and will develop an actionable plan that will help you achieve your goals. Whether Lisa is working with Millennials, business owners, professionals or high net worth executives, all her clients have one thing in common: the desire to go after their goals and make smart financial and life decisions with the help of an experienced professional life coach. She is intimately involved in the Las Vegas area and incredibly determined to make Las Vegas and the world a better place.

www.ADULTINGYOURWAY.com

EPIC AUTHOR PUBLISHING

# GET THE FREE BOOK BONUSES

WWW.ADULTINGYOURWAY.COM

## lisa CHASTAIN

Made in the USA
Middletown, DE
27 December 2018